Geopolitics, China and the Global Supply Chain

In an era of increasing geopolitical turmoil, this book looks at the impact of geopolitics on global supply chains and examines the role of China in East Asia's regional economic integration.

It evaluates the impact of geoeconomic fragmentation along different dimensions such as trade, FDI and capital flows, and provides insights into different industries and sectors where trade and investments are increasingly being reallocated and reshuffled. The book further explores how geopolitics may accelerate the internationalisation of China's renminbi, which herald significant implications for the international monetary system. As geopolitical tensions arising from the US-China trade war continue to persist, the global semiconductor industry has also become the epicentre of US-China strategic rivalry, placing immense strain on its fragmented, global value chain. This book analyses the implications of this intensifying technological rivalry for East Asia, including the ASEAN economies.

This book will be of interest to scholars and students of Asian economics, international trade, and geoeconomics. Policymakers searching for insight into Asian trade and financial markets may also find this book useful.

Sarah Chan is Senior Research Fellow at the East Asian Institute, National University of Singapore. She has previously worked as a senior economist at the Monetary Authority of Singapore and a consultant economist for the Asian Development Bank. She obtained her PhD in Economics from Nanyang Technological University, Singapore in 2014.

Routledge Focus on Economics and Finance

The fields of economics and finance are constantly expanding and evolving. This growth presents challenges for readers trying to keep up with the latest important insights. Routledge Focus on Economics and Finance presents short books on the latest big topics, linking in with the most cutting-edge economics research.

Individually, each title in the series provides coverage of a key academic topic, whilst collectively the series forms a comprehensive collection across the whole spectrum of economics.

International Trade, Regulation and the Global Economy
The Impact of Anti-Competitive Market Distortions
Shanker A. Singham

The Digital Transformation of Banking
Bilal Sucubaşı, Andrijana Bojadzievska Danevska, Savica Dimitrieska and Elena Parnardzieva Stanoevska

The Circular Economy and SMEs
Edited by Fahimeh Khatami

Financial Security and Household Life Insurance
Bridging the Gap
Joanna Dębicka and Anna Jędrzychowska

Corporate Short-Term Financing in Europe
The Role of Trade Credit and Bank Loans in Liquidity Management
Julia Koralun-Bereźnicka

Financial Resilience and the Sustainable Development Goals
Edited by Magdalena Zioło and Bruno S. Sergi

Geopolitics, China and the Global Supply Chain
Issues and Implications
Sarah Chan

For more information about this series, please visit: www.routledge.com/Routledge-Focus-on-Economics-and-Finance/book-series/RFEF

Geopolitics, China and the Global Supply Chain

Issues and Implications

Sarah Chan

Routledge
Taylor & Francis Group
LONDON AND NEW YORK

First published 2026
by Routledge
4 Park Square, Milton Park, Abingdon, Oxon OX14 4RN

and by Routledge
605 Third Avenue, New York, NY 10158

Routledge is an imprint of the Taylor & Francis Group, an informa business

British Library Cataloguing-in-Publication Data
A catalogue record for this book is available from the British Library

ISBN: 978-1-041-14395-6 (hbk)
ISBN: 978-1-041-14396-3 (pbk)
ISBN: 978-1-003-67422-1 (ebk)

DOI: 10.4324/9781003674221

Typeset in Times New Roman
by SPi Technologies India Pvt Ltd (Straive)

Contents

Figures

Tables

1 Is a China-Centric Asian Production Network Still in Existence?

Geopolitical Concerns Gaining Traction Worldwide

Global supply chains have been a key and prominent feature in international trade in the past few decades. Since the early 1990s, technological advances and declining trade barriers have greatly facilitated investment and foreign direct investment (FDI) flows. Rapid innovation in information and communications technology, which vastly reduced transportation costs, and a liberalising trade policy environment have led firms to locate their manufacturing processes across various locations to reap the benefits of specialisation and source for intermediate inputs for production and making goods for export. Exploiting comparative advantages, firms were able to improve the efficiency of most complex manufacturing processes as they engaged in cross-border international trade. These production networks or geographically dispersed global value chains (GVC) contributed to the industrial development of East Asia, which has benefitted from opportunities for growth due to their participation in GVC-related production.

However, the globalisation of supply chains has its own associated costs, apart from the benefits it yields. Firms and countries can be exposed to risks and vulnerabilities in many forms. Extreme weather events (arising from climate change) and natural disasters (such as the 2011 Tohoku earthquake in Japan) had sent shockwaves through global supply chains when the flow of critical inputs was disrupted.[1] Public health shocks like the COVID-19 pandemic have also emerged as a source of risk; in China, closures of port terminals and factory lockdowns due to China's rigorous zero-tolerance COVID-19 policy had not only severely disrupted manufacturing production but also led to spikes in shipping costs as a result of cargo delays.

Geopolitical factors further exposed countries to risks and put the global supply chains under stress. The US-China trade war since 2018 has created uncertainties about China's economic outlook and business environment, and Russia's invasion of Ukraine in February 2022 exposed the

DOI: 10.4324/9781003674221-1

vulnerability of European countries' natural gas supplies. These events underscored the risks of economic interdependence and the importance of economic self-sufficiency. To enhance economic resilience and self-reliance, various countries are implementing policies to boost output and competitiveness of industries deemed critical or strategic. However, these recent industrial policies contain provisions favouring domestic producers at the expense of foreign producers, especially in high-technology industries (Table 1.1). In 2023 alone, there have been 2,500 new industrial policies, of which 71% are trade distortive.[2] These measures have important spillovers through their effects on trade flows. The European Chip Act is an example of localising parts of the supply chain within Europe and reducing reliance on foreign chip supplies.

A surge in trade restriction measures has been evident in recent years. Since 2020, the US and China have stood out as the most active users of quantitative restrictions such as import and export bans, licensing requirements and tariff rate quotas.[3] Geopolitical rivalries have fuelled greater protectionism and use of cross-border restrictions on trade and capital based on national security grounds.[4] The risk of global trade fragmentation would appear to have increased significantly; as trade and capital flows were disrupted, with adverse impact on industrial production and economic activity, firms and policymakers are increasingly looking at strategies to "de-risk" supply chains by moving production back home or to other countries (termed "friend-shoring" or "near-shoring").

Table 1.1 Brief overview of government legislations to bolster countries' positions within the global semiconductor supply chain

United States	The CHIPS and Science Act, signed into law in August 2022, aims to boost US semiconductor research, development and production through US$53bn in chip manufacturing incentives and research investments, as well as an investment tax credit.
EU	First announced in February 2022, the European Chips Act is a €43bn+ investment package that seeks to boost Europe's competitiveness and resilience in semiconductors.
South Korea	South Korea unveiled its "K-Semiconductor Belt Strategy" in May 2021 to build the world's biggest semiconductor supply chain by 2030.
Japan	In 2021, the government released the "Strategy for Semiconductors and the Digital Industry" and approved $7.7bn in funding to support domestic semiconductor manufacturing. In 2022, an additional US$8bn in funding was proposed to bring production hubs for advanced chips to Japan, securing materials for manufacturing and research.
Taiwan	In 2023, lawmakers passed new rules allowing local chip firms to turn 25% of their annual R&D expenses into tax credits as part of efforts to encourage domestic production.

Source: Goldman Sachs, "US-China: More Decoupling Ahead?" Global Macro Research, Issue 118, 1 May 2023.

De-risking or Decoupling amidst Geopolitical Tensions

Before the COVID-19 pandemic, firms had begun de-risking strategies to diversify from China. Some production stages in China's supply chains, particularly labour-intensive processes, had migrated to lower-cost locations such as Indonesia and India because of China's rising labour costs over the past decade. Since 2018, this reconfiguration process has been accelerated by heightened trade tensions between the two superpowers. There is anecdotal evidence that some South Korean firms have shifted from China or stopped expanding their operations in the People's Republic; LG Electronics for instance, moved all production of US-bound refrigerators at a facility in Zhejiang province to South Korea, in an attempt to circumvent US sanctions on Chinese exports.[5]

Samsung and SK Hynix, which have major memory chip production facilities in China,[6] have reportedly stated it will invest more in the United States since they cannot mass produce cutting edge chips without US equipment and technology. Samsung, for example, is investing tens of billions of dollars in advanced chip manufacturing in Texas due in part to generous subsidies from the United States.[7] This is in response to the United States' export controls on 7 October 2022 prohibiting companies (including those outside the United States) from selling semiconductors to China if they were manufactured using US software and equipment. Although Korean firms have secured temporary exemptions from the rules, the uncertainties have led the companies to invest more at home for cutting edge production rather than to continue investing in China.[8]

Elsewhere, firms are also recalibrating their plans to mitigate supply chain risks by reducing over-exposure to China. Dell has announced that it will phase out all China-made chips by 2024 and asked its suppliers to significantly reduce other "made in China" components in its widely popular laptop and desktop computers and servers.[9] In addition to moving more production to Vietnam, Dell is eyeing increased production in India and Mexico, among other places. Other companies are following suit. Taiwan's Foxconn, best known for assembling Apple's iPhones, is building new plants and adding production capacity to India. Foxconn's engagement in India will be on manufacturing semiconductors and other electronic components. The percentage of iPhones that Foxconn assembles for Apple in India is estimated to increase to 25%–30% by the end of 2025.[10] This represents a substantial shift in production out of China to India. Beyond India, Foxconn is also outsourcing its manufacturing to Vietnam and Mexico, alongside India while its operations in China continue to decline.[11] Apparently, the move to diversify away from China has gained urgency in the midst of mounting geopolitical headwinds.

The continued US-China trade tensions risk disrupting global supply chains. The US Senate passage of the BIOSECURE Act in 2024, which sought to prohibit federally funded US pharmaceutical companies from contracting with specific enterprises within the biopharmaceutical supply chain, has created a chilling effect on Chinese biotech firms. In late December 2024, Wuxi AppTec, which has 65% of its revenue derived from the US market, announced the sale of its cell and gene therapy manufacturing units in the United States and the United Kingdom to American investment firm Altaris.[12] In retaliation against US sanctions targeting China's strategic industries and tightening restrictions on advanced chips and technologies to China, China expanded its export control of rare earths on 9 October 2025, requiring firms to obtain government approval to ship magnets that contain trace amounts of Chinese-origin rare earth materials or that produced using Chinese mining, processing, or related technologies. Given China's dominance and near monopoly on extracting rare earths as well as refining them, global supply chains would be adversely affected. In Europe, aviation companies such as Airbus, carmakers like Volkswagen and electric vehicle producers (including Tesla) will be hit hard by shortages of rare earths. Firms in defence industries would encounter constraints on components while in sectors like semiconductors, American firms such as Nvidia, Intel and Apple are likely to experience rising costs and production delays from rare earth shortages. Taiwan's chipmaker, TSMC, could see its chip sales to US firms affected as it needs rare earths for the production of AI semiconductors. The escalating US-China trade tensions have inadvertently created uncertainties and led to a more volatile global economic environment.

Supply Chain Reshuffling across Sectors and Economies

The deterioration in US-China trade relations has far-reaching implications for economies around the world given the integrated nature of global supply chains. Over the years, China has rapidly moved up the value chain and enhanced its domestic production capabilities, playing a crucial role in integrating the region's economies as it emerged as a hub around which global trade networks are configured.

Given that the global Input-Output table comes with a time lag,[13] making it ill-suited to examine the shifts in global supply chains over the past five years, this analysis draws on disaggregated data from the UN Comtrade which has the advantage of being up to date while providing a reasonable level of detail on products at the SITC and HS (Harmonised Commodity Description and Coding System) levels.

The disaggregated trade data at the SITC 7 level showed that China was adversely affected by the tariffs from the trade war with the United States, suffering a sharp 9.5 percentage-point decline in its market share of US imports (Figure 1.1). Conversely, Vietnam saw the largest gain in market share of 3.1 percentage points, followed by Mexico with 2.8 percentage

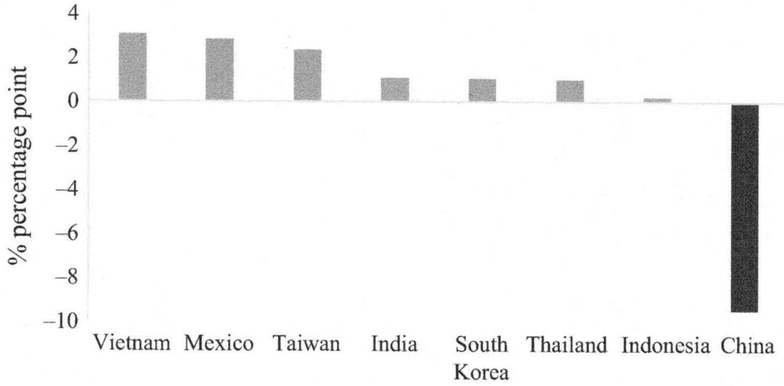

Figure 1.1 Change in US import market shares for machinery and transport equipment (SITC 7), 2017–2023.

points, and Taiwan, with 2.4 percentage points. Vietnam is a major beneficiary of production relocation from China, similar to Mexico, which also gained significantly from the trade diversion, given its proximity to the United States and favourable tariff treatment under the US-Mexico-Canada Agreement. The trade diversion to Taiwan reflects the reshoring of production lines and its competitive strengths in higher value-added upstream products. Meanwhile, Thailand and Indonesia registered modest gains of 1 percentage and 0.2 percentage points in their respective shares of US imports of machinery and auto products.

The discernible shift from China as a source of US imports is also evident across a wide range of traded goods. Figure 1.2 visually presents the shifts in import market share within four sectors that are often central to US trade – automobiles, auto parts, electronics and semiconductors. The decline in China's share in US imports after 2017 is apparent in all categories, while Taiwan and Vietnam have seen their shares in US imports increase in the electronics and semiconductor categories, with Vietnam making the most gains except in auto parts and vehicles (where imports by the United States from Vietnam are negligible).

In semiconductors, high-income economies in Asia, such as Taiwan, have seen a notable increase in their market share, whereas for Mexico, it has benefitted from exporting automobiles and electronics to the United States. Mexico's electronic sector is geared more towards downstream production (i.e. processing and assembly of products for final goods) even though it has had considerable success in attracting lower value-added production. It has less success with drawing investments in higher value-added upstream electronics manufacturing, in part reflecting its relatively unskilled workforce and weak supporting infrastructure.

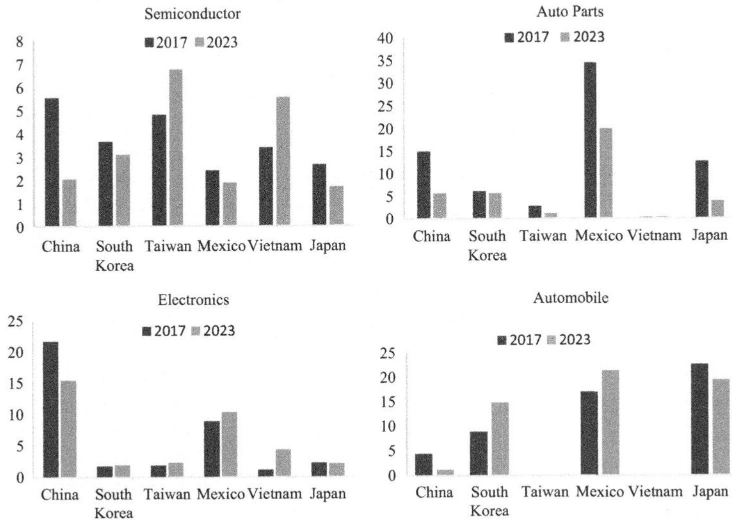

Figure 1.2 Market shares of US imports of machinery and transportation goods (%).

Source: UN Comtrade.

Figure 1.3 shows that foreign investments in China have, in fact, been on the decline since 2011. This is not driven by a fall in FDI from the United States alone, but by a broad-based decline from virtually all major FDI source countries into China, including major Asian economies (Japan, Korea and Taiwan) and the United Kingdom. This suggests that the underlying causes are factors domestic to China which were in place even prior to the US-China trade tensions. These likely include rising wages or restrictions on foreign ownership (such as joint venture requirements) or concerns over intellectual property protection.

Heightened geopolitical tensions can transmit via financial linkages, not merely through trade; however, this has not been borne out of data for the past few years, given it could still be too early to assess the spillover effect from the US-China decoupling or de-risking. However, preliminary data suggest that portfolio inflows into China had started to turn negative and declined by more than US$100 billion in 2022 (Figure 1.4), reflecting the continued trade tensions between the United States and China, as well as a host of other factors such as a slowing Chinese economy and widening interest rate differentials with other major economies. Although portfolio inflows gradually stabilised in the subsequent years (Figure 1.4), continued US-China trade rivalry has adversely affected the investment climate in China.

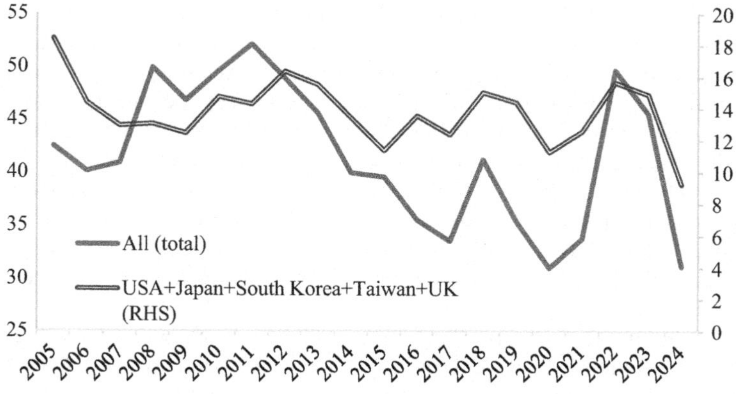

Figure 1.3 FDI in China (US$ billion), 2005–2024.

Source: CEIC database.

Note: Utilised FDI.

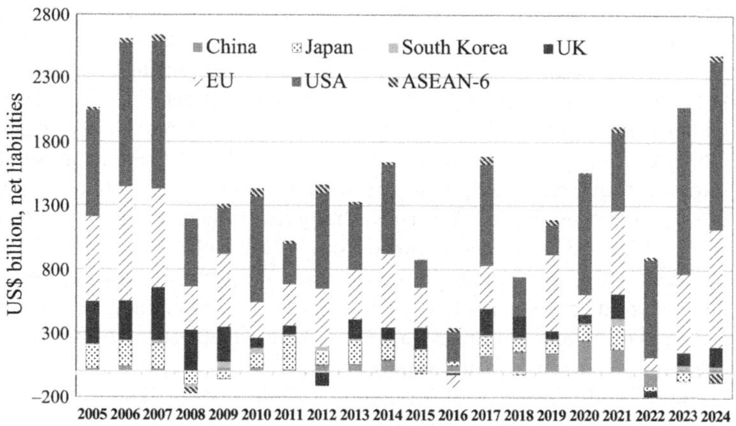

Figure 1.4 Portfolio inflows into China and selected countries, 2005–2024.

Source: IMF, CEIC database.

Geoeconomic fragmentation arising from increased geopolitical rivalries and conflicts has adverse repercussions not just for China and the United States, but for the global economy.[14] There is evidence that trade patterns are shifting as firms respond to growing policy uncertainty and look for ways to insulate their supply chains from geopolitical risks. However, despite diversification by companies to move away from China, supply chains, particularly those involving Chinese suppliers and American consumers, have lengthened instead of shortened during December 2021 and September 2023.[15]

In a recent research study by the Bank for International Settlements, there are now more *indirect links* between customer firms and overseas suppliers "as new firm nodes interpose themselves into existing supply chains".[16] For instance, while China remains a key location for Apple's manufacturing operations, the iPhone and iMac maker is increasingly diversifying production and suppliers towards India and Vietnam. This would likely show up as an increase in the number of indirect links between Apple and its overseas supplier firms in China and other parts of Asia. Thus, despite US-China decoupling with intermediate goods production shifting to other countries in Asia, China remains integral to global supply chains.

Findings further show that China is still very much integrated with the Asian economies, particularly Taiwan and Vietnam, despite signs of China decoupling from the United States. Its economic ties with Mexico (given the latter's proximity to the US market and participation in a trade bloc with the United States and Canada) have also been intensifying, even if the United States has been moving away from China as a source of imports since the US-China trade war. China's share in US imports declined from 22% in 2017 to 15% in 2023, and recent research suggests that unofficial non-tariff barriers were responsible for 50% of the overall reduction in Chinese imports from the United States during the height of the US-China trade war in 2018 and 2019.[17] Between 2017 and 2023, China made substantial gains in its share in Vietnam's imports by around 6.5 percentage points during this period.[18] For Mexico, the share of its imports from China had grown considerably from 1% in 1994 to 18% in 2017 and 20% in 2023. Conversely, the proportion of Mexico's imports from the United States had declined from 72% in 1994 to 48% in 2017 and to 44% in 2023. As China's exports to these countries comprise intermediate parts and components that are then assembled into final goods for the US market, China continues to be a significant player in the upstream stages of US manufacturing supply chains.

Based on the patterns of foreign direct investment (FDI) which serve as a mode through which firms can structure and organise their activities in the global value chain (GVC),[19] there are indications that Chinese firms have been expanding their FDI activities in lower-cost locations, through which they remain potentially connected to US production chains. Vietnam is a case in point. Chinese outward investment in Vietnam had nearly tripled to US$2.2 billion in 2021 from US$764 million in 2017.[20] Similarly, China's outbound FDI in Mexico has also risen, with China's direct investment in Mexico's manufacturing sector growing fivefold from US$31.6 million in 2017 to US$151.5 million in 2022.[21] Close to three quarters of this FDI between 2017 and 2022 was in two industries that are significant in GVCs, namely computer and peripheral equipment and motor vehicle parts.[22] Thus, despite a decline in US import sourcing from China, there has been an increase in China's import share in US "friend-shoring" nations like Vietnam and Mexico. This suggests that China may continue to play a significant role in US supply chains and global production network, with the United States' indirect supply chain links to China remaining intact.

China's Centrality in Asian Trade and Production Network

Apparently, China still plays a pivotal role in the division of labour within regional production networks. Reflecting growing cross-border trade within regional supply chains, the ASEAN-6 economies have increased their imports of capital goods and auto/transport components from China since 2010, rising from 9% to 12% in 2017 and 13% in 2023 (Table 1.2). Among ASEAN countries, Vietnam has seen the greatest intensification of electronics industry linkages with China due to investment from South Korea and increasingly from China, which outsource the production of electronics peripherals and components to Vietnam. China is also sourcing more electrical parts like integrated circuits from foreign semiconductor plants established in Vietnam; accordingly, Vietnam's share in China's imports of intermediate capital goods rose from near zero in 2010 to 6% in 2017, albeit registering a slight increase to 4% in 2023 (refer to Table 1.2).

The ASEAN-6 economies collectively accounted for 13% of China's total imports of intermediate electrical inputs in 2023 (Table 1.2). Malaysia, Thailand, the Philippines and Malaysia are major suppliers of hard disk drives to the China-centric production network, given the presence of top global manufacturers including Western Digital, Seagate, Hitachi and Toshiba in the ASEAN region.

Japan, South Korea and Taiwan are China's upstream suppliers of materials, parts and components which are used extensively as inputs into China's downstream manufacturing assembly activity. These three economies respectively accounted for 14%, 8% and 7% of China's imports of capital machinery goods in 2023, though the share of all three East Asian economies had somewhat fallen over the years from 2010 to 2023 (Table 1.2). Japan's exports of various electronics products have registered declines in the past decade while over the same period, the global share of South Korea's exports of mobile phones had likewise slumped from about 12% in 2010 to less than 2% in 2023.[23]

In the final capital goods category, China was badly hit by US tariffs, suffering a sharp 5.4 percentage-point decline in its market share of US imports. Correspondingly, the share of the United States in China's exports had fallen from 2017 to 2023 (refer to Table 1.2), even though China remained an important major source of final machinery and transport products and continued to supply more than half of US imports. China is more of an exporter of machinery and auto parts to the EU than an importer.

Table 1.2 China's trade in capital goods and transport equipment (% share of world total), selected years

Country/region	*2010*		*2017*		*2023*	
	Intermediate (parts and components)	*Finished/final*	*Intermediate (parts and components)*	*Finished/final*	*Intermediate (parts and components)*	*Finished/final*
Exports						
USA	13.5	19.9	16.8	23.0	12.7	17.6
EU	18.8	18.7	12.3	16.5	19.1	16.0
Japan	7.3	5.0	6.6	5.2	4.6	4.5
South Korea	5.8	3.5	4.8	3.7	4.7	2.4
Taiwan	3.3	1.3	2.2	1.3	2.3	1.3
ASEAN-6	8.5	7.8	11.5	8.3	13.1	10.9
Singapore	2.9	2.5	1.9	2.0	1.5	2.5
Malaysia	1.9	1.4	1.5	1.2	2.2	1.7
Indonesia	1.0	1.3	1.3	1.3	1.8	1.8
Philippines	0.7	0.5	0.8	0.8	0.8	1.0
Thailand	1.2	1.1	2.2	1.3	2.3	1.8
Vietnam	0.9	1.0	3.8	1.6	4.5	2.1
Imports						
USA	5.6	9.5	6.9	14.8	5.0	11.0
EU	11.0	23.2	19.1	24.1	13.5	29.2
Japan	16.7	19.4	16.2	17.4	14.1	17.4
South Korea	15.7	11.9	11.3	8.5	8.1	5.2
Taiwan	14.8	9.4	7.7	7.3	7.3	6.9
ASEAN-6	15.6	8.8	14.3	9.7	13.4	14.1
Singapore	2.3	1.3	1.2	1.9	1.5	3.3
Malaysia	8.0	1.8	2.3	1.8	4.1	3.1
Indonesia	0.3	0.3	0.3	0.3	0.4	0.4
Philippines	2.4	1.6	1.5	1.3	1.4	1.0
Thailand	2.3	3.5	3.3	2.5	2.4	3.1
Vietnam	0.3	0.3	5.7	1.8	3.6	3.2

Source: UN Comtrade database.

Regional Interdependencies of Electronics Supply Chains

A recent IMF paper found that the shift in US imports away from China may not have reduced dependence on China. The decoupling in trade between the United States and China may only serve to obscure the indirect linkages between the United States and China through the industrial supply chains of their partners. In particular, countries that were more deeply engaged in China's supply chains (i.e. had more intense intra-industry trade with China) including Vietnam, Taiwan and Mexico experienced significant rises in export market shares in the United States from 2017 to 2022.[24]

Figure 1.5 shows that China remains highly integrated with the East Asian region, despite the US-China trade dispute. China is still a key player in the global and regional production network as measured by the Grubel-Lloyd index,[25] which is used to assess China's intra-industry trade (IIT) in various disaggregated levels in the SITC 7 category of machinery and transportation (M&T) industry. Since the 2008 Global Financial Crisis, the IIT index had steadily risen until 2017, when it declined from 0.61 to 0.56 in 2022, possibly suggesting some shifting/diversification of activities away from China's trade in M&T with East Asia. In general, the IIT index in the trade of electrical and auto machinery had remained stable at around 0.56 in 2002 and 2022, indicating that China is still deeply involved in the East Asian region.

This further supports IMF findings that countries which have benefitted from rapid export growth to the United States are also deeply engaged in supply chains with China via IIT. To further examine the shifts and

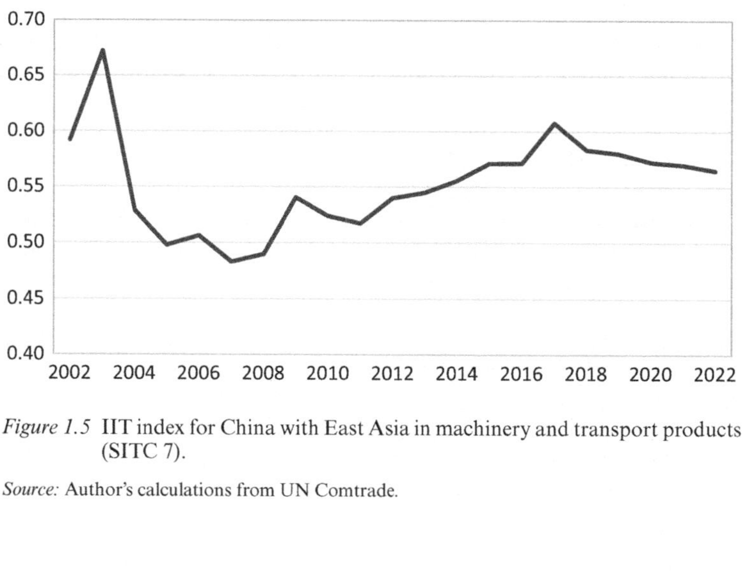

Figure 1.5 IIT index for China with East Asia in machinery and transport products (SITC 7).

Source: Author's calculations from UN Comtrade.

changes taking place in China's trade with East Asia, IIT indices are calculated for various disaggregated levels of the information and communication technology (ICT) industry that comprise mainly intermediate goods such as the related parts of computers, mobile phones and electronics. A full list of categories included in the ICT product classification based on the HS codes at the four- and six-digit level can be found in Appendix 1.1. These division codes are compiled from the UN's definition of machinery and electrical equipment under the ICT industry.[26]

In China's IIT at the disaggregated level of the ICT industry, China's trade with East Asia is dominated by particular types of intermediate goods. Appendix 1.2 reports the sectors with rising IIT indices and those with index higher than 0.5. Among East Asian economies, China is most integrated with Taiwan, with high IIT indices (>0.5) in 13 ICT sectors, compared to only seven each for South Korea, Malaysia and the Philippines, eight for Thailand, six each for Vietnam and Indonesia, and four for Singapore.

China's IIT with Taiwan is diversified and integrated in office machinery parts (HS 844399, HS 847321 and HS 847330) but more so in the semiconductor sector (HS 8533, HS 8534, HS 8435, HS 8536, HS 8537, HS 8538, HS 8541 and HS 8542). Taiwan is central to the global chip industry's international division of labour. Despite importing many key manufacturing inputs from around the world, it has built a highly integrated supply chain of factories, design firms, silicon wafer and specialty chemical makers, APT (Assembly, Packaging and Testing) plants and universities that churn out engineers and technicians for the industry.[27] Today, it dominates the market for logic chips in the advanced nodes (10 nm or below) which are required for computer-intensive devices and smartphones.[28]

Trade between China and Korea from 2017 to 2022 focused on some electronic components, with rising indices reported in sectors such as HS 8534, HS 8535, HS 8536, HS 8538 and HS 8541. On the other hand, IIT indices have declined in some sectors such as video recording, office printing machinery (HS 8522, HS 844399 and HS844340) and electrical resistors (HS 8533).

Among ASEAN countries, a high IIT index of 0.7 and 0.9 was respectively reported for semiconductors (HS 8541) and electronic integrated circuits (HS 8542) in China's trade with Singapore, which hosts facilities for outsourced assembly and testing companies as well as manufacturing facilities for top contract foundries. Bilateral trade in this sector has been driven by China's demand for semiconductors and the machinery for manufacturing them.

Reflecting China's domestic production capabilities in a range of a final electronics goods, China's imports from the rest of ASEAN countries are mainly peripherals that include audio/visual-related products

(HS 8522 and HS 8521) or parts that go into the manufacturing of computers, TV, mobile phones and so on. As Appendix 1.2 shows, China's IIT with Thailand and Philippines is highly integrated in office equipment like photocopiers (HS 844399) and parts of automatic data processing machines like hard-disk drives (HS 847330) and certain electronic components (HS 8536, HS 8540 and HS8541).

Further, China's IIT with Malaysia experienced increases in several sectors such as IT and telecom equipment including audio/visual-related products (HS 8519, HS 8522 and HS 847330) and electronic components (HS 8536, HS 8538 and HS 8519), compared to Indonesia's (HS 8522, HS 8533, HS 8536 and HS 8541).

Due to global demand for smartphones that require memory chips (DRAM and flash memory), ICT industries such as sound recording apparatus (HS 8519) and other electrical devices (HS 8536, HS 8537, HS 8541 and HS 8542) experienced significant growth in China's bilateral trade with Vietnam. Vietnam has emerged as a significant player in the global and regional supply chain due to its competitive labour costs and growing manufacturing capabilities; its GVC participation has been growing significantly, on average by 13.3% per annum in the period 2010–2020.[29] A newcomer to the multinational production network, Vietnam specialises in the assembly stage of the value chain, which is reflected in the high reliance of its exports on imported intermediate inputs; half of the value added in Vietnam's exports originated from abroad in 2020.[30]

Reallocation rather than De-globalisation

China has emerged as a key player in the global manufacturing supply chain over the past two decades. Its accession to the World Trade Organisation (WTO) in 2001 and the liberalisation of its FDI and trade policies in the early 2000s have boosted exports and facilitated the country's integration into the world economy, allowing it to play a pivotal role in global production and trade networks. However, supply chain shocks from the COVID-19 pandemic and geopolitical tensions, particularly the US-China trade war, have heightened concerns about the over-reliance of supply chains on China. This prompts firms to diversify and countries to try to reorganise their production activities to mitigate supply chain risks. To reduce dependence on China, the United States is pursuing policies in favour of "friend shoring" or "near shoring" (notably Mexico) or reshoring.

This leads to the question of whether China could still retain an integral role in global supply chains given that the United States' direct economic engagement with China through trade and FDI has been declining, especially since 2017. The shifting of US imports away from China may not have reduced dependence on China as much as import numbers suggest because countries that were more deeply engaged in Chinese supply chains experienced the most rapid export growth with the United States. In particular, there is evidence (using highly disaggregated trade data) to show that countries that saw faster export growth with the United States in certain sectors like electronics and machinery also had more intense IIT with China in those same sectors. For instance, Appendix 1.2 shows that Vietnam had intense IIT with China in various types of electrical and electronic equipment (HS 8537, HS 8541 and HS 8542), and this corresponds with higher US market share of imports from Vietnam in these categories (refer to Figure 1.2).

Apparently, China remains highly integrated with East Asia in the machinery and electronics industries, and while it may not replicate the strategy adopted by other countries (like Japan in the 1970s and 1980s) to set up production in the United States (via horizontal FDI) to circumvent government restrictions and cater to the American market, it is nonetheless increasing its investment in countries that export more to the United States. This implies that the United States may *de facto* remain dependent on China through third countries, including Vietnam and Mexico.

Further, the World Bank's Hirschman Herfindahl (HH) index shows that Vietnam experienced the most rapid rise (>40%) compared to other Asian economies like Malaysia or Thailand whose market concentration index increased by more than 10% to 20% during the 2017–2022 period. Vietnam's increased market concentration is driven by more intense trade relationships with both China and the United States – Vietnam saw its share of US exports rose from 20% to 30% from 2017 to 2022, while also importing more from China, from 26% of its total imports in 2017 to 33% in 2022.

Over the years, China's manufacturing base has deepened, registering an increase in domestic production of components within the global production networks. It has become competitive across a wide spectrum of goods in global export markets and increasingly moving up the value chain. More of its exports now come from domestic firms, rather than foreign-invested enterprises, whose share in China's exports had declined to 31% in 2022 from 58% in 2005. This suggests that Chinese firms are raising their technological level. China appears to have enhanced its domestic production capabilities, with processing exports progressively reducing the use of imported inputs and replacing them with domestically produced materials.[31]

The upshot is that China may well remain entrenched in the global supply chain and given its well-developed ecosystem of strong network of suppliers, manufacturers and relatively skilled and adaptable labour force, it may not be easy to move supply chains out of China. Manufacturers are now performing more supply chain activity within China, supported by digitalisation at home. Chinese producers are also dominating some aspects of the supply chain, notably solar cell manufacturing. China's share in all the manufacturing stages of solar panels exceeded 80% in 2021.[32] It also accounts for 75% of the world's battery cell manufacturing capacity, due to its control of the supply of critical materials for lithium-ion batteries.[33] The same is true for rare earth metals needed to produce wind turbines, which are 80% controlled by China.[34] China is likely to remain as the world's manufacturing hub given its status as one of the world's largest markets that enjoys sufficient demand and economies of scale to attain optimal efficiency levels in production.

Appendix 1.1 Harmonised System (HS) classification of ICT goods

Categories	*HS code 2017*
(I) **Office Machines**	
Calculating machines; electronic calculators capable of operating without an external source of electric power and pocket-size data recording, reproducing and displaying machines with calculating functions	847010
Other calculating machines; electronic and non-electronic	847021, 847029, 847030
Cash registers	847050
Machines incorporating a calculating device	847090
Duplicating machines	847210
Machines for sorting, folding and opening mail	847230
Office machines, n.e.s.	847290
Printing machinery	844331, 844332
Parts thereof	
Machinery; parts and accessories (other than covers, carrying cases and the like) of the machines of heading no. 8472	847340
Calculating machines; parts and accessories of the electronic calculating machines of item no. 8470.10, 8470.21 or 8470.29	847321
Printing machinery; parts and accessories	844399
(II) **Telecom Products**	
Telephone sets	851711, 851712, 851718
Microphones and stands therefor	851810
Loudspeakers, mounted in their enclosures	851821, 851822
Loudspeakers, not mounted in their enclosures	851829
Headphones, earphones and combined microphone/speaker	851830
Audio-frequence electric amplifiers	851840
Electric sound amplifier sets	851850
Transmission apparatus	852550
Transmission apparatus with reception apparatus	852560
Television cameras, digital cameras and video camera recorders	852580
Radar apparatus, radio navigational aid apparatus and radio remote control apparatus	8526

(*Continued*)

Appendix 1.1 (Continued)

Categories	*HS code 2017*
Monitors and projectors, not incorporating television reception apparatus; reception apparatus for television, whether or not incorporating radio-broadcast receivers or sound or video recording or reproducing apparatus	8528
Parts thereof	
Microphones, headphones, earphones, amplifier equipment; parts of the equipment of heading no. 8518	851890
Transmission apparatus; parts suitable for use solely or principally with the apparatus of heading no. 8525 to 8528	8529
Sound recording or reproducing apparatus	8519
Video recording or reproducing apparatus	8522, 8521
(III) **IT Products**	
Automatic data processing machines and units thereof, magnetic or optical readers, machines for transcribing data onto data media in coded form and machines for processing such data, not elsewhere specified or included	8471
Parts thereof	
Machinery; parts and accessories (other than covers, carrying cases and the like) of the machines of heading no. 8471	847330
(IV) **Semiconductors/Electronic Components**	
Printed circuits	8534
Electrical resistors (including rheostats and potentiometers), excluding heating resistors	8533
Electrical apparatus for switching, protecting electrical circuits, for making connections to or in electrical circuits and for a voltage exceeding 1,000 volts	8535
Electrical apparatus for switching and protecting electrical circuits, for making connections to or in electrical circuits, for a voltage not exceeding 1,000 volts; connectors for optical fibres, optical fibre bundles or cables	8536
Boards, panels, consoles, desks, cabinets, bases with apparatus of heading no. 8535, 8536 for electricity control and distribution (other than switching apparatus of heading no. 8517)	8537
Electrical apparatus; parts suitable for use solely or principally with the apparatus of heading no. 8535, 8536 and 8537	8538
Thermionic, cold cathode or photo-cathode valves and tubes (e.g. vacuum, vapour, gas-filled valves and tubes, mercury arc rectifying valves and tubes, cathode-ray and television camera tubes)	8540
Diodes, transistors, similar semiconductor devices; including photovoltaic cells assembled or not in modules or panels, light-emitting diodes and mounted piezo-electric crystals	8541
Electronic integrated circuits	8542

Source: Compiled by author.

Appendix 1.2 IIT indices for China with East Asian Economies (selected years)

	Partner Economy	*HS code*																
		844399	*847321*	*847340*	*851890*	*8529*	*8519*	*8522*	*847330*	*8534*	*8533*	*8535*	*8536*	*8537*	*8538*	*8540*	*8541*	*8542*
Korea	2003	0.0	0.54	0.10	0.17			0.76	0.77	0.21	0.62		0.55	0.49	0.30	0.21	0.66	0.18
	2017	0.58	0.07	0.97	0.81			0.83	0.49	0.53	0.96	0.09	0.57	0.98	0.69	0.55	0.76	0.24
	2022	0.41	0.0	0.26	0.76			0.45	0.37	0.76	0.31	0.67	0.72	0.99	0.75	0.36	0.84	0.43
Singapore	2003	0.0				0.61				0.97			0.92	0.76	0.98		0.57	0.44
	2017	0.91				0.56				0.95			0.60	0.63	0.53		0.57	0.73
	2022	0.66				0.30				0.33			0.52	0.34	0.42		0.74	0.90
Malaysia	2003	n.a.		0.10	0.44	0.61	0.58	0.57	0.70				0.87	0.43	0.78	0.74		0.10
	2017	0.41		0.59	0.74	0.77	0.48	0.79	0.77				0.81	0.62	0.65	0.63		0.29
	2022	0.51		0.21	0.43	0.23	0.72	0.87	0.86				0.97	0.31	0.88	0.21		0.58
Thailand	2003	0.0				0.34			0.77	0.62			0.41	0.79	0.66	0.78	0.18	
	2017	0.71				0.99			0.63	0.93			0.88	0.60	0.99	0.22	0.41	
	2022	0.80				0.99			0.92	0.78			0.90	0.44	0.83	0.51	0.93	
Indonesia	2003	n.a.						0.67			0.50		0.81		0.73		0.42	0.08
	2017	0.76						0.51			0.19		0.47		0.69		0.49	0.32
	2022	0.56						0.72			0.71		0.73		0.67		0.70	0.48
Philippines	2003	n.a.		0.0		0.45		0.72	0.41	0.87			0.0	0.07	0.79	0.87	0.10	
	2017	0.81		0.57		0.57		0.56	0.38	0.95			0.72	0.54	0.21	0.34	0.20	
	2022	0.84		0.72		0.44		0.14	0.58	0.55			0.95	0.28	0.22	0.84	0.57	
Vietnam	2003	n.a.	n.a.				n.a.			0.21	0.64		0.17	0.07			0.53	0.10
	2017	0.65	0.97				0.41			0.51	0.93		0.51	0.26			0.65	0.80
	2022	0.95	0.27				0.73			0.43	0.11		0.54	0.93			0.89	0.87
Taiwan	2003	0.18	0.12		0.90				0.91	0.19	0.38	0.14	0.59	0.13	0.51	0.99	0.94	0.60
	2017	0.53	0.58		0.82	0.34		0.07	0.68	0.45	0.63	0.32	0.92	0.84	0.73	0.61	0.62	0.53
	2022	0.78	0.62		0.26	0.70		0.67	0.85	0.94	0.53	1.0	0.60	0.66	0.89	0.90	0.78	0.54

Source: Author's calculations based on UN Comtrade database, Taiwan's MOF (https://portal.sw.nat.gov.tw/APGA/GA03E) (accessed 28 October 2023).

Notes

1 Christoph E Boehm et al., "Input linkages and the transmission of shocks: Firm-level evidence from the 2011 Tohoku earthquake", *Review of Economics and Statistics*, 101(1), 2019.
2 Evenett et al., "The return of industrial policy in data", International Monetary Fund Working paper wp/24/1, 2024.
3 Gary Clyde Hufbauer and Ye Zhang, "Limits to trade quantities are making a comeback", *Peterson Institute of International Economics*, July 2025.
4 The ongoing shift in production against the backdrop of the US-China trade or technology war is reflective of geo-economic fragmentation – a policy-driven reversal of global economic integration often guided by strategic considerations. See Aiyar Shekhar, Andrea Presbitero and Michele Ruta. "Geoeconomic Fragmentation and the Future of Multilateralism", *IMF Staff Discussion Notes*, 15 January 2023b.
5 Françoise Nicolas, "Reshuffling value chains – South Korea as a case study", *Asie Visions*, No. 135, Ifri, April 2023.
6 Samsung Electronics has a NAND flash memory factory in Xi'an and a test packaging factory in Suzhou, while SK Hynix has a fab (a microchip manufacturing plant) in Wuxi, near Shanghai, that produces DRAM chips for other companies, and a NAND flash memory (formerly an Intel) factory in Dalian. Samsung uses its facilities in China to produce 40% of its NAND chips, one of two kinds of memory chips that help devices store data. SK Hynix produces 30% of its NAND chips in China and almost half of its DRAM chips. *The New York Times*, "What the U.S.-China Chip War Means for a Critical American Ally", 27 September 2023, https://www.nytimes.com/2023/09/27/business/samsung-hynix-south-korea.html (accessed 4 November 2023).
7 Martin Chorzempa, "How US chip controls on China benefit and cost Korean firms", *Peterson Institute for International Economics*, Policy Brief, July 2023.
8 Martin Chorzempa, "How US chip controls on China benefit and cost Korean firms", *Peterson Institute for International Economics*, Policy Brief, July 2023.
9 *Nikkei Asia*, "Dell looks to phase out 'made in China' chips by 2024", https://asia.nikkei.com/Spotlight/Supply-Chain/Dell-looks-to-phase-out-made-in-China-chips-by-2024.
10 "Trump wants America to make iPhones: Here's how India is doing it", *The New York Times*, 30 June 2025.
11 "Taiwan's Foxconn and others accelerate investment in Mexico", *NikkeiAsia*.https://asia.nikkei.com/Spotlight/Supply-Chain/Taiwan-s-Foxconn-and-others-accelerate-investment-in-Mexico.
12 Reva Goujon and Juliana Bouchaud, "The clawback: Reclaiming strategic assets from China, *Rhodium*, 31 March 2025.
13 The World Input-Output database extends up to 2014 while the OECD Inter-Country Input-Output Tables are available up till 2018.

14 A recent literature review of empirical studies focusing on geoeconomic fragmentation concludes that existing research puts the costs of fragmentation in the range of 0.2%–7.0% of GDP, and even up to 12% if technological decoupling is included. Refer to source in Footnote 11.

15 BIS researchers examined data from more than 25,000 companies and found that the average distance between supplier firms and customer firms increased from 9.67 in December 2021 to 10.03 in September 2023. Han Qiu, Hyun Song Shin and Leanne Si Ying Zhang, "Mapping the realignment of global value chains", *BIS Bulletin*, October 2023.

16 Han Qiu, Hyun Song Shin and Leanne Si Ying Zhang, "Mapping the realignment of global value chains", *BIS Bulletin*, October 2023.

17 Tuo Chen, Chang-Tai Hsieh, and Zheng Michael Song, "Non-tariff trade barriers in the U.S.-China trade war", BFI Working Paper, No. 2022-99, Becker Friedman Institute China, University of Chicago, 2022.

18 The proportion of China inputs in Vietnam's imports rose from 27.5% in 2017 to 34% in 2023. Author's calculations from CEIC database.

19 FDI can either function as a complement or substitute to trade whereby firms can cater to the market through an alternative "mode" by engaging in horizontal FDI (i.e. setting up plants in the foreign country and directly selling to the foreign market instead of exporting). However, Chinese firms are unlikely to use such a mode (to set up production bases in the United States) given the prevailing geopolitical climate.

20 CEIC database.

21 Laura Alfaro and Davin Chor, "Global supply chains: The looming "Great Reallocation", NBER Working Paper, No. 31661, September 2023.

22 Laura Alfaro and Davin Chor, "Global supply chains: The looming "Great Reallocation", NBER Working Paper, No. 31661, September 2023.

23 Calculations from data extracted from UN Comtrade database.

24 From 2017 to 2022, countries with the biggest gains in market share in the United States were Vietnam (1.9 ppt), Taiwan (1 ppt), Canada (0.75 ppt), Mexico (0.64 ppt), India (0.57 ppt) and Korea (0.53 ppt). These six countries more than account for China's 5.3 percentage point decline. See Freud et al., "Is US Trade Policy Reshaping Global Supply Chains?" IMF draft, May 2023.

25 The Grubel-Lloyd index varies between 0 (indicating pure *inter*-industry trade) and 1 (indicating pure *intra*-industry trade). Once a country's export and import values for a particular sector and period are known, it is calculated as $GL_{\text{sector i}} = 1 - \left(\frac{\left| \text{export}_{\text{sector i}} - \text{import}_{\text{sector i}} \right|}{\text{export}_{\text{sector i}} + \text{import}_{\text{sector i}}} \right)$.

26 Refer to United Nations, "Measuring trends in ICT Trade: From HS2002 to HS2007/ICT Product Definition", 10 May 2011. https://unstats.un.org/unsd/classifications/ExpertGroup/EGM2011/AC234-23.PDF (accessed 26 August 2023).

27 "Jeremy Mark and Dexter Tiff Roberts, "United States-China semiconductor standoff: A supply chain under stress", *Atlantic Council*, 23 February 2023.
28 Boston Consulting Group and Semiconductor Industry Association, *Strengthening the Global Semiconductor Supply Chain in an Uncertain Era*, April 2021.
29 GVC participation is measured as the sum of foreign value added in exports and domestic value added in other economies' exports.
30 WTO, World Trade Report 2023: Re-globalisation for a secure, inclusive and sustainable future.
31 Hiau Looi Kee and Heiwai Tang, "Domestic value added in exports: Theory and firm evidence from China", *American Economic Review*, 106(6), 1402–1436, 2016.
32 International Energy Agency, "Solar PV Global Supply Chains", IEA Special Report, July 2022.
33 BloombergNEF.
34 Alicia G Herrero, "Resilience of Global Supply Chains: Facts and Implications", ADB Working Paper, June 2023.

2 ASEAN and China

Shifting Trade Dynamics amid US-China Trade Rivalry

Enhanced Trade and Foreign Direct Investment Linkages

A salient feature in the economic development of the Association of Southeast Asian Nations (ASEAN) has been the important role of foreign trade in driving economic growth. Over the past few decades, ASEAN economies (particularly Singapore, Malaysia, Thailand, Indonesia and the Philippines), which by nature are very open and outward-looking, have become one of the world's most dynamic regions. This dynamism is largely due to strong export growth, fuelled by substantial foreign investment.

Trade relations between China and ASEAN are influenced mainly by the growth and expansion of both economies, and China's drive towards economic modernisation. In part due to the geographical proximity and historic relations with China, ASEAN's economic linkages with the Mainland via trade, investment and tourism have increased significantly over the past few decades. China rapidly became a major trading partner of ASEAN economies particularly after its entry into the World Trade Organisation in 2001. It has been ASEAN's top trading partner since 2009, with bilateral trade growing by 9.2% year-on-year, reaching US$734 billion in 2024.[1]

In a way, China had been crucial to ASEAN's growth during the 2008–2009 Great Financial Crisis. China's efforts to maintain currency stability by re-pegging the yuan to the dollar (from October 2008 to June 2010) provided an anchor of stability to the region. Its countercyclical macroeconomic policies also helped to cushion against the economic fallout from a worldwide recession. By implementing a four-trillion-yuan stimulus package, China successfully lessened the impact of the 2008–2009 global downturn on its economy, thus stabilising regional demand for imports from ASEAN countries, particularly commodities.

ASEAN's economic relations with China have grown and thrived from the dynamism of their economies and the liberalisation of their trade regimes. Driven by China's emergence as a global manufacturing centre as well as regional trading agreements such as the ASEAN-China

DOI: 10.4324/9781003674221-2

Free Trade Area, ASEAN member states are becoming more economically integrated with mainland China. As China becomes a capital-surplus economy, its investment in ASEAN has also grown apace. Since the onset of the US-China trade war, the share of ASEAN-6 in China's outward investment had risen to 12.6% in 2023, a significant leap from 8.3% in 2018 (Figure 2.1).

Chinese firms have become globally diversified and are venturing overseas in pursuit of natural resources and seeking business opportunities in the region particularly as labour costs/wages rise in the Mainland. Apart from manufacturing, Chinese firms are also actively investing in ASEAN's digital economy (i.e. e-commerce, fintech), establishing multiple data centres[2] across the region to cater to the demand from cloud computing clients (Figure 2.2).

Some tech companies like Alibaba and ByteDance are also reportedly training their artificial intelligence models in Southeast Asia's data centres to access Nvidia's chips, apart from servicing their overseas customers and growing their share of the global cloud computing market.[3]

In addition, major Chinese telecommunication companies such as Huawei, China Telecom, China Mobile and ZTE, for instance, are developing digital infrastructure such as 5G networks across the region. China views ASEAN countries as important markets for its "friend-shoring" strategies particularly as rivalry between the United States and China further intensifies.

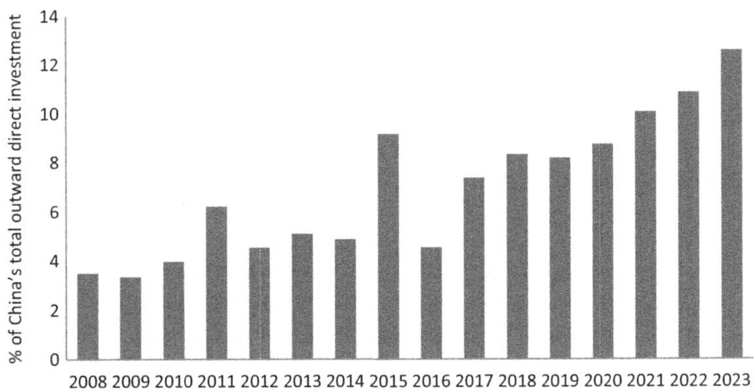

Figure 2.1 China's outward investment to ASEAN-6, 2008–2023.

Source: CEIC.

Note: ASEAN-6 refers to Singapore, Malaysia, Thailand, Indonesia, the Philippines and Vietnam.

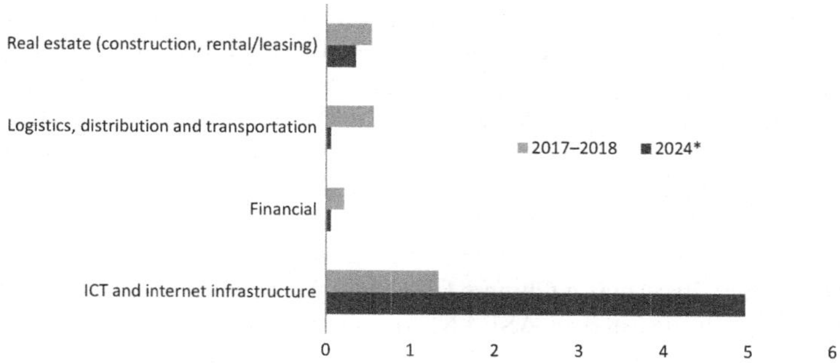

Figure 2.2 China's announced Greenfield investment in ASEAN-6 (US$ billion).

Source: fDi Markets.

Note: ICT and internet infrastructure = data centres, cloud computing, e-commerce, 5G and Internet of Things. Data as of October 2024.

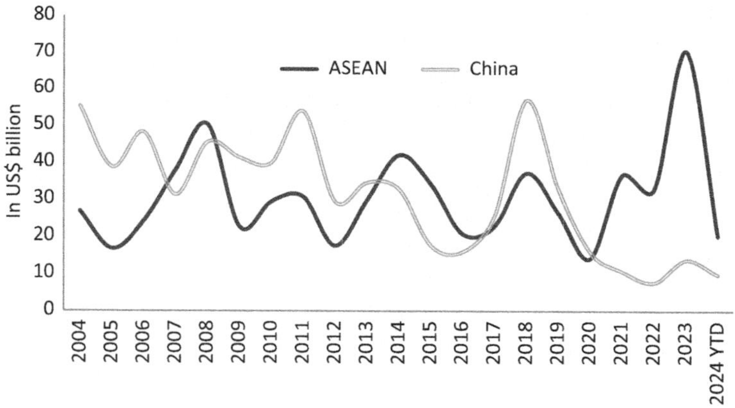

Figure 2.3 Greenfield FDI in ASEAN-6's manufacturing sector.

Source: fDi Markets.

Note: YTD = year to date. Till August 2024.

Amid supply chain challenges driven by geopolitical tensions, foreign firms seeking to de-risk or diversify their operations away from China have begun redirecting some of their investments to ASEAN. ASEAN has become a key target region for multinational firms adopting a China+1 strategy to reduce reliance on China, particularly in the wake of the COVID-19 pandemic. Since 2021, ASEAN has overtaken China as a destination of choice for manufacturing investment from the Organisation of Economic and Development economies (Figure 2.3).

Given the ongoing supply chain diversification, the five largest ASEAN economies (Indonesia, Thailand, Singapore, Vietnam and Malaysia) accounted for approximately 96.5% of manufacturing FDI pledged to the region in 2022 and 2023, according to fDi Markets database. In 2023, China's investment in ASEAN-6's manufacturing sector surpassed the investment from the United States and was more than triple that of South Korea and Japan (Figure 2.4). Notably, the electric vehicle (EV) sector has attracted significant investment from Chinese firms. Since 2019, major Chinese EV Original Equipment Manufacturers have actively invested in ASEAN, focusing on the production of EVs and batteries. For instance, BYD's extensive investments in the region encompass EV production, components and charging stations while Dongfeng Motor began production of EV sports utility vehicles in Thailand in 2023.[4]

As geopolitical tensions continue to escalate between the United States and China, China has stepped up its economic engagement with ASEAN. However, this also exposes the bloc to possible risk of collateral damage. For instance, if major economies impose extensive levies on Chinese EVs, some of ASEAN's intermediate exports to China used as inputs for EV production could be impacted. It is therefore in ASEAN's interest to diversify and promote further economic linkages with other countries via

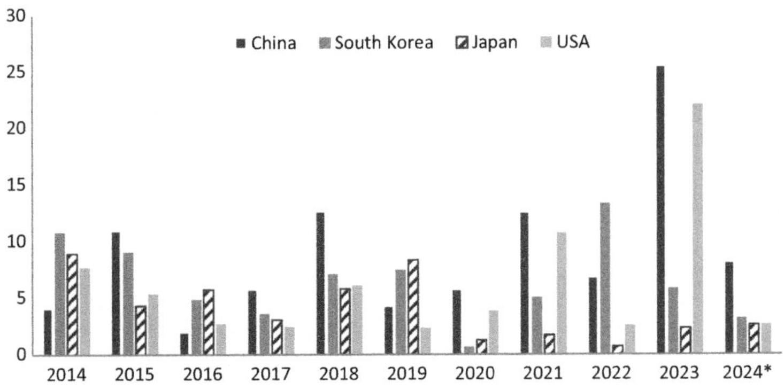

Figure 2.4 Announced Greenfield investment in ASEAN-6's manufacturing (in US$ billion).

Source: fDi Markets.

Note: * denotes year to date (August 2024).

the Regional Comprehensive Economic Partnership (RCEP) to enhance supply chain resilience especially given heightened supply chain vulnerabilities and geopolitical uncertainties.

ASEAN-6's Positioning amid the US-China Trade Dispute

Figure 2.5 shows that China was adversely affected by the tariffs from the trade war with the United States, suffering a sharp 9.7 percentage-point decline in its market share of US imports. In contrast, Vietnam saw the largest gain in market share of 3 percentage points, followed by Thailand with 1 percentage point and Malaysia with 0.3 percentage point. This could primarily be due to rerouting by companies in China to Vietnam as an intermediate route for their US exports to avoid tariffs on Chinese products. Notably, Vietnam is a major beneficiary of production relocation from China, given its well-trained labour force and relatively well-developed infrastructure and open environment.[5]

Malaysia is another key beneficiary of supply chain shifts amidst the US-China trade war. As the world's sixth largest semiconductor exporter and responsible for 13% of the global semiconductor packaging, assembly and testing market, Malaysia is attracting an increasing number of Chinese semiconductor design companies which are tapping on Malaysian firms to assemble a portion of their high-end chips, as they are

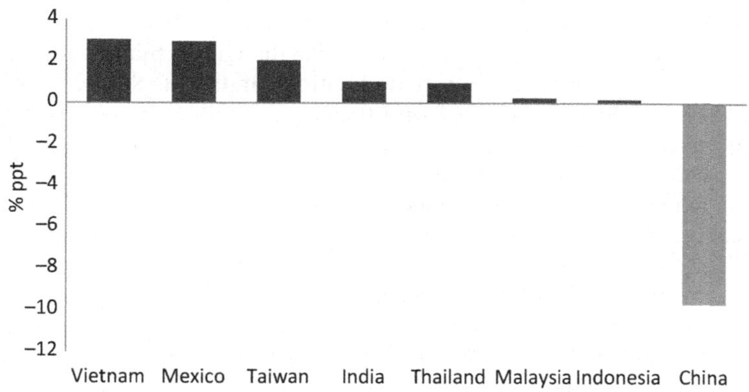

Figure 2.5 Change in US import market shares for capital machinery and transport equipment, 2017–2023.

Source: UN Comtrade.

keen to mitigate risks in the event of further US sanctions on China's chip industry. US restrictions do not currently apply to advanced chip packaging services but some Chinese firms are reportedly de-risking by partnering with Malaysian firms to assemble a portion of their high-end chips as advanced packaging of chips can significantly improve chip performance and is emerging as a critical technology in the semiconductor industry.[6]

To the extent that ASEAN serves as a connector of trade between China and the United States, the ASEAN region has grown in importance as an integral node in global value chains, as both a manufacturing hub and a significant player in the technology supply chain network. Table 2.1 shows that the ASEAN-6 economies[7] import more intermediate goods from China than the export of intermediate products. The ASEAN-6 countries have increased their intermediate imports of capital goods and auto/transport components from China since 2010, with the share substantially rising from 13% to nearly 20% in 2017 and 27% in 2023.

In contrast, the share of the United States and other East Asian economies (specifically, Japan, South Korea and Taiwan) in ASEAN-6's imports had declined over the 2010–2023 period. ASEAN-6 is more of an exporter than importer of intermediate goods from the United States. Prior to the US-China trade war, the United States accounted for only 10% of ASEAN-6's intermediate exports in 2017, but this jumped by nearly 11 percentage points to 21% in 2023. For finished machinery goods, the increase in export share gain was approximately 13 percentage points, with the United States accounting for 28% of ASEAN's exports in 2023. These shifts in trade shares reflect the increasing importance of the ASEAN-6 as an upstream and downstream producer for major economies like the United States and as an increasingly important export destination for China. Suffice to say, ASEAN is highly integrated with the global production network with its backward and forward linkages and active participation in the machinery and automotive industries.

Evidently, the increase in import shares in the United States of ASEAN countries such as Vietnam, Thailand and Malaysia (Figure 2.5) is accompanied by an increase in the share of China's exports to those countries. From 2017 to 2023, the gain in the share of China's exports to Vietnam was 0.6 percentage point, while the increase in the share of China's exports to Malaysia and Thailand was 0.5 percentage point and 0.4 percentage point, respectively.[8]

These shifts in trade patterns have been complemented by foreign direct investment (FDI) reallocation, whereby countries such as Vietnam, Malaysia and Thailand experienced a recent increase in an inflow of Chinese investment. For instance, foreign-registered capital in Vietnam

Table 2.1 ASEAN-6's trade in capital goods and transport equipment (% share of world total), selected years

Country/region	*2010*		*2017*		*2023*	
	Intermediate (parts and components)	*Finished/final (capital machinery)*	*Intermediate (parts and components)*	*Finished/final (capital machinery)*	*Intermediate (parts and components)*	*Finished/Final (capital machinery)*
Exports						
China	12.2	11.1	14.8	9.4	10.6	10.2
USA	9.3	16.0	10.3	15.7	21.2	28.4
East Asia (Japan, South Korea and Taiwan)	17.1	12.0	16.9	13.9	15.2	12.4
Imports						
China	13.0	26.5	19.6	32.8	26.9	39.6
USA	14.1	11.6	10.5	8.3	13.7	8.3
East Asia (Japan, South Korea and Taiwan)	33.2	24.0	37.2	22.5	24.0	16.7

Source: UN Comtrade.

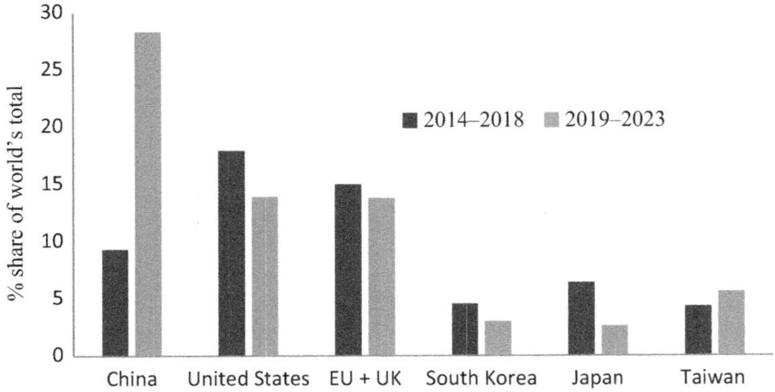

Figure 2.6 FDI in ASEAN-6's semiconductor and electronics component industries, 2014–2023.

Source: fDi Markets.

from China rose by 22% from 2017 to reach US$2.6 billion in 2022.[9] Approved investment in Thailand from China almost quadrupled from US$1 billion in 2018 to US$3.6 billion in 2023.[10] Figure 2.6 shows that the FDI share of China in ASEAN-6 economies in the semiconductors and electronics components industries had surged to almost 30% in the 2019–2023 period, from 9% in the five years prior to the 2018 US-China trade war when it first started. In contrast, the share of investment from the United States, the European Union and the United Kingdom in the chips and electronics sectors of ASEAN economies has declined.

These findings corroborate those in a World Bank report[11] which reveals that the increase in the share of China's FDI outflows to a country is positively correlated to an increase in its share of US imports. Concomitantly, an increase in the share of Chinese FDI outflows to a country is positively correlated to an increase in its share of Chinese imports.

ASEAN-6's increased intermediate goods trade with China in a way can be attributed to China's industrial upgrading. As China rapidly manifests growing comparative advantage in manufacturing, it has become a major global supplier of industrial inputs, with PRC-made inputs accounting for around 3% of world output in 2018.[12] China's rapid ascent up the manufacturing value-added ladder implies that its industrial structure is increasingly complementary to that of ASEAN, while becoming more competitive with major economies like the United States. This is

Table 2.2 China's trade complementary index with ASEAN-6, the USA, Japan and South Korea (2018 and 2023)

	2018	*2023*
Singapore	60.9	63.1
Indonesia	60.1	65.0
Malaysia	68.4	72.1
Thailand	65.0	69.5
Philippines	65.5	66.0
Vietnam	67.1	72.3
USA	68.0	67.9
Japan	63.9	60.8
South Korea	64.4	62.9

Source: WITS, World Bank.

reflected in the rise in trade complementary indices (TCI)[13] with ASEAN-6 economies, alongside a decline in TCI with Japan, South Korea and the United States (Table 2.2).

Within the EV industry in ASEAN, the rise in trade complementarity between some ASEAN member states and China is evident. Chinese production and exports of EV parts and EVs began to rise rapidly only after 2020.[14] Table 2.3 lists the sectors that comprised more than or close to 20% of ASEAN's exports to China during the period from 2022 to 2023. Evidently, the export shares of ASEAN-6 countries to China in battery materials like lithium cathode (an essential ingredient in the manufacture of EV batteries) are sizeable, ranging from 26% of Singapore's exports to more than 50% for Malaysia, Thailand, the Philippines and Vietnam.[15] Singapore exports slightly more than a quarter of lithium-ion batteries to China (27%) while Indonesia is the biggest exporter of these EV batteries among ASEAN countries, with 60% of its total exports of EV batteries shipped to China. Thailand, widely known as the automotive hub in the ASEAN grouping, shipped slightly more than half of its EVs (52%) to China.

Further, there is even higher trade complementarity between ASEAN and China in critical minerals, which are vital in the manufacture and production of EV parts and vehicles. Table 2.3 reveals that ASEAN's shipments of critical materials show a high degree of export concentration to China. Around 93% of Malaysia's cobalt exports and 95% of the country's manganese ore are destined for the China market.

Table 2.3 ASEAN-6's exports to China within the EV supply chain (% share)

Country	*Critical minerals (unrefined or processed)*			*Manufacturing of parts*				*Product*
				Battery materials		*Cell components of batteries/ battery packs*		
	Cobalt (HS 810520)	*Manganese ore (HS 260200)*	*Nickel ore (HS 260400)*	*Lithium cathode (HS 284290)*	*Graphite cathode (HS 854519)*	*Lithium-ion batteries (HS 850760)*	*Electric battery module for EV (HS 850790)*	*Electric vehicle (HS 870240)*
Singapore (2022–2023)				25.9		27		
Malaysia (2022–2023)	93.3	94.7		57.6		18.6		
Indonesia[b] (2022)						60.4		
Thailand (2022–2023)				50.1	37.4			51.8
Philippines (2022–2023)			97.1	51.8				
Vietnam (2022–2023)				57.9			20.8[a]	

Source: Author's calculations from UN Comtrade.

Note: EV parts include HS tariff lines 850760 (lithium-ion batteries), 850790 (battery parts) and 850132 (electric motors).

[a] denotes the latest available data for the year 2022.

[b] Indonesia banned the export of nickel ore in 2020. Only processed nickel such as ferronickel and nickel pig iron is allowed to be exported.

The Philippines, a major supplier of nickel ore, exported 97% of its nickel to China. Indonesia, rich in nickel ore reserves, has been progressively banning the export of nickel ore since 2022.[16] It has however attracted investment from China to bolster its mining and refining capabilities. Chinese firms have reportedly poured US$14 billion over the past decade to secure nickel supplies for the development of the EV industry.[17]

China's EV-related investment in ASEAN has increased particularly amid ongoing US-China trade rivalry. Nio, listed on the Singapore Exchange in 2022, announced plans to set up an R&D centre in Singapore for artificial intelligence and autonomous driving (refer to Appendix 2.1). SAIC initiated a US$15 million industrial park in Thailand in 2023 to expand its EV capacity in ASEAN.[18] The investment includes a factory for battery modules and other EV components. Chery announced in 2022 a U$1 billion investment for EV and battery production, and R&D facilities in Indonesia.[19] Further, in 2023, Changan invested an initial US$285 million in EV and battery production in Thailand.[20] Chinese auto manufacturers are making inroads into the Southeast Asian market, with their dominance in the EV industry largely attributed to vertical integration across the entire battery supply chain, from the acquisition of raw materials to the production of batteries.

Challenges amid a Changing Geopolitical Landscape

ASEAN's economic integration with China exposes the region to uncertainties amid the US-China trade war. While the ASEAN-6 economies have positioned themselves as attractive production alternatives for companies seeking to relocate manufacturing away from China and have gained from trade diversion in terms of increased exports to the United States, they also face the risk of experiencing potential negative impacts of the US-China trade conflict. For instance, ASEAN's exports to China are at risk of increased duties slapped on China's EVs or other goods such as chips. Singapore's electronics sector will be negatively impacted as around 36.3% of its machinery for manufacturing semiconductor/chip (HS code 848620) was exported to China from 2022 to 2023. Semiconductors are critical components in electronics manufacturing and utilised as inputs in the EV industry. Singapore and Malaysia's exports of processors and memory chips could suffer collateral damage if the US-China trade war escalates.

The United States and China are ASEAN's major trading partners and will remain the biggest sources of external shocks to ASEAN over the medium term. The US-China trade decoupling or de-risking is leading to a bifurcation in trade, particularly in technology-related products.

By January 2021, average US tariffs on imports from the PRC were 19.3%, more than six times higher than before the US-China trade war began in 2018. The tariffs affected 66.4% of US imports of China's products. Likewise, China's retaliatory tariffs on US imports also remained high at 21%, affecting 58.3% of imports from the United States.[21] ASEAN's heavy reliance on trade exposes the Southeast Asian region to profound uncertainty due to the ongoing trade and technological conflict between the two major powers. This presents a formidable challenge as the ASEAN region relies heavily on a stable global environment to sustain growth.

ASEAN economies therefore need to carefully calibrate their strategies, given their significant exposure and vulnerability to current geopolitical developments. Measures by the United States, such as the countervailing and anti-dumping duty investigations of photovoltaic cell imports from Cambodia, Malaysia, Thailand and Vietnam using components from China, are indicative of more future stringent policies to contain indirect trade through connector countries such as Vietnam.[22] China's Trina Solar, for instance, received a dumping margin of 77.85% for the solar panel products it makes in Thailand and 54.46% for those it produces in Vietnam.[23]

Under a second Trump administration, the United States may tighten rules of origin to reduce China's value-added contributions in exports from trading partners like Vietnam. This could include tariffs on countries with growing trade surpluses, such as Vietnam. In response, Vietnam might adopt a more market-oriented exchange rate policy and aim to limit its current account surplus with the United States to no more than 5% of GDP.[24] On 2 July 2025, the United States and Vietnam announced a trade deal incorporating a "transshipment" clause, which imposes a 40% tariff on goods merely routed through Vietnam to the United States without substantial local processing. This measure has sparked concerns for China's regional and global supply chains, given Vietnam's deep integration into Chinese production networks and heavy reliance on Chinese intermediate imports. As of September 2025, the exact definition of "transshipment" and implementation details remain unclear, contributing to ongoing uncertainty.

If content-based rules of origin are enforced – subjecting Vietnamese goods with significant Chinese content to higher tariffs – multinational firms might employ transfer pricing strategies, which follow established rules and standards to ensure appropriate profit allocation for tax purposes, to adjust the reported values of intermediates shipped between affiliates and thereby meet local content thresholds. However, such approaches would complicate enforcement for authorities, as verifying true value-added shares in multinational-controlled supply chains is both complex and resource-intensive. Overall, the threat of punitive tariffs on products with high Chinese content could discourage foreign direct investment in Vietnam. In a worst-case scenario, further tightening of rules to target goods from Chinese-owned firms could severely disrupt China's supply chains and broader Asian economies.

At a time when the US-China relationship is poised to deteriorate due to a hawkish Trump administration, ASEAN countries should further upgrade its technological capabilities to rely less on foreign inputs in order to avert trade restrictive measures like tariffs. Strategies to mitigate exposure and vulnerability to geopolitical developments should focus on building supply chain resilience. In the case of Vietnam, although firms have yet to shift their manufacturing operations, some foreign businesses could turn cautious and reconsider possible new investments as Vietnam is reliant on components and parts imported from China. Phipps International reportedly had to close a factory that manufactures medicine cabinets and mirrors as it could not find reliable local parts suppliers compared to those from China.[25]

Balancing between the major powers is proving to be challenging. Vietnam's "bamboo diplomacy" (i.e. firm but flexible approach to foreign policy) and Malaysia's neutral stance could be difficult to maintain as geopolitical tensions rise. Vietnam, for instance, seeks to balance relations by upgrading its relationship with the United States to a "strategic partnership" without entering into military alliances, while reaffirming its ties with China through initiatives like the "Community of Shared Future".[26] Other countries like Malaysia are using sub-regional cooperation platforms, such as the Brunei Darussalam–Indonesia-Malaysia–Philippines East ASEAN Growth Area Vision 2025 and the Indonesia-Malaysia-Thailand Growth Triangle Vision 2036 to promote multilaterialism and intra-regional trade.

Expanding trade relationships beyond the United States and China might reduce dependency risks in industries that could be heavily impacted by these tensions. Southeast Asian countries are cooperating with regional partners to mitigate the fallout from the US-China trade war. The aim is to expand relationships by bolstering economic ties with other regional and global trade partners, such as through the RCEP, to help mitigate the adverse effects of future escalating trade tensions in a fragmenting global economy.

Appendix 2.1 List of China's announced Greenfield investments in ASEAN-6

Recipient country	*Investing firm*	*Project date*	*Sector*	*Activity*	*Investment (US$ million)*
Indonesia	Contemporary Amperex Technology (CATL)	Nov 2020	Electronic components (batteries)	Manufacturing	5,100
	CNGR Advanced Material	Apr 2021	Non-ferrous metal production and processing	Manufacturing	330
	WM Motor	Sep 2021	Automotive OEM	Sales	11.3
	Weiming Group	Nov 2021	Non-ferrous metal production and processing	Manufacturing	400
	Zhejiang Huayou Cobalt Nickel Materials	Apr 2022	Copper, nickel, lead and zinc mining	Extraction	253.9
	Huatuo International	Jun 2022	Non-ferrous metal production and processing	Manufacturing	2604
	GEM Energy Materials	May 2023	Non-ferrous metal production and processing	Manufacturing	500
	Huayou International Mining	May 2023	Non-ferrous metal production and processing	Manufacturing	200
	Chery Automobile	Jul 2023	Automotive OEM	Manufacturing	255.7
	Tsingshan Holding Group	Aug 2023	Non-ferrous metal production and processing	Manufacturing	587.4
	Zhejiang Hozon New Energy Automobile (Hozon Auto)	Jan 2024	Automotive OEM	Manufacturing	296.9
	BYD	Jan 2024	Automotive OEM	Manufacturing	1000
	Rept Battero	Mar 2024	Electronic components (batteries)	Manufacturing	362.7
	Tianneng Power International		Electronic components (batteries)	Sales	2.6

Singapore	NIO (Next EV)	May 2022	Automotive OEM	R&D	94.4
	Zhejiang Geely Holding Group (Volvo)		Software and IT services	R&D	28.3
	Li Auto	Nov 2023	Semiconductors	R&D	89
	Eve Energy	Dec 2023	Electronic components (batteries)	Sales, marketing	2.6
Thailand	Shanghai Automotive Industry Corporation	Jan 2022	Electronic components (batteries)	Manufacturing	14.7
	BYD	Sep 2022	Automotive OEM	Manufacturing	491.5
	Gotion High-tech Co. Ltd	Dec 2022	Electronic components (batteries)	Manufacturing	17.3
	Zhejiang Hozon New Energy Automobile (Hozon Auto)	Mar 2023	Automotive OEM	Manufacturing	204.6
	Great Wall Motors	Mar 2023	Electronic components (batteries)	Manufacturing	30
	Changan Automobile Group	Apr 2023	Automotive OEM	Manufacturing	286
	Guangzhou Automobile Industry Group	Jun 2023	Automotive OEM	Assembly, manufacture of EVs	31.9
	Chery Automobile	Jul 2023	Automotive OEM	Manufacturing	204.6
	Rongtai Electric Material	May 2024	Non-metallic mineral products	Manufacturing	41
	Zhejiang Geely Holding Group (Volvo)	Jul 2024	Automotive OEM	Sales, marketing	11.3
Malaysia	Eve Energy	May 2023	Electronic components (batteries)	Manufacturing	422.4
	Wanbang Digital Energy	May 2023	Electronic components (i.e. EV charging equipment)	Providing smart electric-charging technology solutions	2.6
	Chery Automobile	Jul 2023	Automotive OEM	Manufacturing	104.2
	Shenzhen Senior Technology Material	Aug 2023	Electronic components (separators for lithium-ion batteries)	Manufacturing	684.8
	Shenzhen Xixin Electronic Technology	Nov 2023	Electronic components (batteries)	Manufacturing	1.8
	Zhejiang Hozon New Energy Automobile	Jan 2024	Automotive OEM	Manufacturing	104.2
	Gotion High-tech Co. Ltd	Aug 2024	Electronic components (batteries)	Manufacturing	198.1

(*Continued*)

Appendix 2.1 (Continued)

Recipient country	*Investing firm*	*Project date*	*Sector*	*Activity*	*Investment (US$ million)*
Philippines	Yadea Group Holdings	Jun 2023	Electric motorcycle	Manufacturing	1000
Vietnam	Gotion	Nov 2022	Electronic components (batteries)	Manufacturing	275
	BYD Auto	Jan 2023	Automotive components	Manufacturing	250
	Vietnam Yadea Electric Motorcycle Company	Aug 2023	Electric motorbikes	Manufacturing	110.1
	Chery Automobile	Apr 2024	Automotive OEM	Manufacturing	800
	Talway (subsidiary of Shanghai Greatway Electric Group)	May 2024	Electronic components (batteries)	Manufacturing	700
	Dongguan Tailing Electric Vehicle	Aug 2024	Electric motorbikes	Manufacturing	67

Source: fDi Markets database.

Notes

1 CEIC database.
2 More than 25 data centres in ASEAN are ultimately owned by Chinese companies. *ASEAN Investment Report 2024*.
3 "China's tech giants take AI model training offshore to tap Nvidia chips", *Financial Times*, 27 November 2025.
4 *ASEAN Investment Report 2024*: ASEAN Economic Community 2025 and Foreign Direct Investment.
5 In electronics, Vietnam has succeeded in attracting big technology firms. Samsung was an early entrant in 2014, investing more than US$600 million in a manufacturing plant. Since then, its investments have attracted its own suppliers to open plants. Apple and Xiaomi also moved some production to the country. These investments helped Vietnam rise in electronics, computers and component exports, making it the 10th largest electronics exporter in 2020. However, as Vietnam focuses on the assembly of finished products for export – with components and design done elsewhere – value added remains low. "ASEAN and Global Value Chains: Locking in Resilience and Sustainability", Asian Development Bank, March 2023.
6 Seeking to limit China's access to high-end GPUs that could fuel artificial intelligence breakthroughs or power supercomputers and military applications, Washington has increasingly placed restrictions on their sales as well as on sophisticated chip-making equipment. As those sanctions bite and an AI boom fuels demand, smaller Chinese semiconductor design firms are struggling to secure sufficient advanced packaging services at home. Some of the Chinese companies are interested in advanced chip packaging services, as advanced packaging of chips can significantly improve chip performance and is emerging as a critical technology in the semiconductor industry. "Chinese firms look to Malaysia for assembly of high-end chips, sources say", Reuters, 19 December 2023.
7 Singapore, Malaysia, Thailand, Indonesia, Vietnam and the Philippines.
8 Data calculated from UN Comtrade.
9 Data calculated from CEIC database.
10 Data from CEIC database.
11 World Bank East Asia and the Pacific Economic Update, October 2024.
12 China's production of intermediate manufactured goods has advanced even more rapidly than its production of final goods. Baldwin et al., "Hidden exposure: Measuring U.S. supply Chain reliance", *BPEA Panel*, Washington, 28 September 2023.
13 Trade complementarity measures the extent to which the export profile of the reporter country complements or matches the import profile of the partner country. A value of the trade complementarity index closer to 100 indicates that trade complementarity exists between country *i* and country *j*, and a value closer to zero indicates that no complementarities are present in trade.

14 Historically, Chinese vehicles were not significant competitors in the major car producing economies like the United States, Japan, South Korea and the EU. However, China is emerging as a leader in the EV and hybrid vehicle trade, with exports increasing 537% from 2018 to 2022, to just under a million EVs exported in 2022 (the largest volume for any exporter). Refer to Coffin et al., "The impact of changes in trade policies on the Electric Vehicle (EV) sector: A CGE Analysis", The US International Trade Commission, Economics Working Paper 2024–05–A, May 2024.

15 Vietnam has abundant nickel deposits and has the potential for mineral exploitation in the production of lithium-ion battery. Blackstone Minerals, an Australian-owned exploration and mining company, is reportedly developing an integrated upstream (mining) and downstream (refining) battery metals processing business in northern Vietnam with the aim of producing nickel-cobalt-manganese precursor products for Asia's growing lithium-ion battery industry. https://theinvestor.vn/northern-vietnam-nickel-mining-project-globally-significant-australian-envoy-d8776.html (accessed 6 November 2024).

16 Indonesia produced an estimated 40.2% of the world's nickel in 2023, according to S&P Global Market Intelligence data.

17 "Chinese companies are flocking to Indonesia for its nickel", *Bloomberg*, 15 December 2024.

18 A Special ASEAN Investment Report 2023.

19 A Special ASEAN Investment Report 2023.

20 A Special ASEAN Investment Report 2023.

21 Chad P Bown, "The US-China trade war and phase one agreement", *Journal of Policy Modeling*, 43(4), 805–843, 2021.

22 Refer to source in Endnote number 11.

23 On 29 November 2024, the United States announced that it would set dumping duties of between 21.31% and 271.2%, depending on the company, on solar cells from Cambodia, Malaysia, Thailand and Vietnam. "US sets tariffs for solar panels from South-east Asian nations", *The Straits Times*, 30 November 2024.

24 Nguyen Xuan Thanh, "Vietnam: Navigating the geopolitical tension with a new industrial policy", presentation at the *EAI Joint Conference "Navigating Challenges: Industrial Policy, Competitiveness and Development"*, held in Singapore from 9 to 10 January 2025.

25 "Vietnam Won Big in Donald Trump's First Trade War Now, it's a Target", *Wall Street Journal*, 16 December 2024.

26 Refer to source in Endnote 24.

3 Internationalisation of the Renminbi

Driven by Geopolitics or Economics?

How Far Has RMB Internationalisation Progressed?

The renminbi (RMB) surpassed the Japanese yen in November 2023 to become the fourth most active currency behind the US dollar (48%), euro (22%) and pound sterling (7%) in international payments. According to the data from the Society for Worldwide Interbank Financial Telecommunication (SWIFT), there has been a rise in the share of the RMB in global payments over the past years, from 1.9% in 2019 to 3.8% in December 2024 (Figure 3.1).

The rise in share reflects the Chinese government's policy actions to raise yuan usage (such as allowing and facilitating the RMB to be used to settle trade) and countries seeking alternatives to the dollar. Figure 3.2 shows that the cross-border share of the RMB for trade settlements and financing has risen sharply since 2022, coinciding with Russia's invasion of Ukraine. Russia's increasing use of the RMB to evade US financial

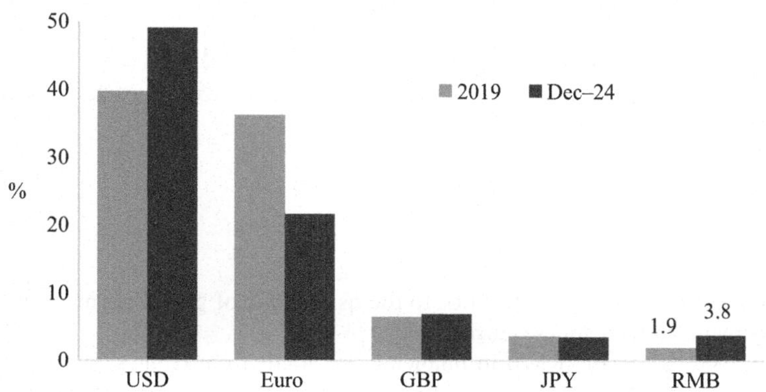

Figure 3.1 Share of major currencies in international payments (%).

Source: RMB Tracker (SWIFT).

DOI: 10.4324/9781003674221-3

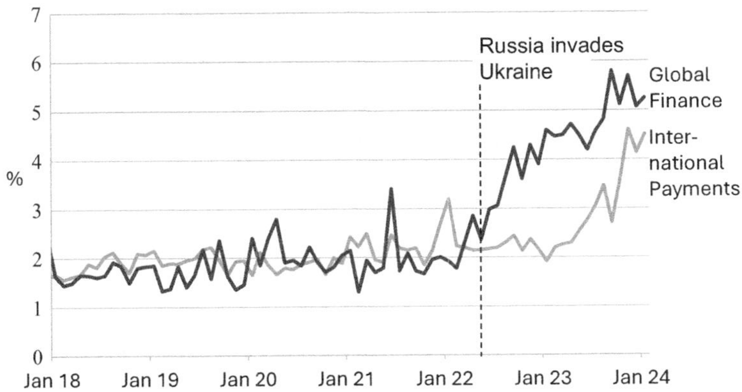

Figure 3.2 Share of RMB in international payments and global finance (%).

Source: SWIFT.

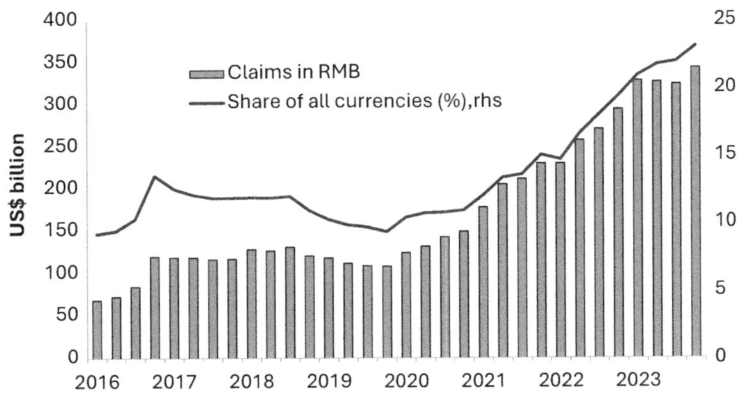

Figure 3.3 Foreign claims of China's banks.

Source: CEIC.

sanctions has likely contributed to the rising share of global payment settlements in the Chinese currency.

The use of the RMB in financing (i.e. loans from Chinese banks or issuing of RMB-denominated bonds) remains strong due to elevated US interest rates and higher dollar funding costs. The RMB is increasingly playing an important role in Chinese banks' cross-border claims, particularly overseas loans[1] (Figure 3.3). However, as an investment currency, the

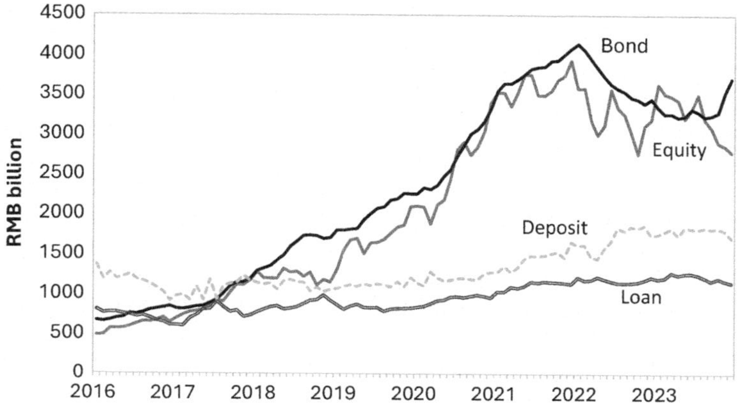

Figure 3.4 Foreign holdings of domestic RMB assets.

Source: CEIC.

RMB is not making much headway. There has been some sell-off in foreign holdings of RMB assets like securities and particularly of bonds since 2022 due to the interest rate hikes by the US Federal Reserve to rein in inflation (Figure 3.4).

The higher usage of RMB in international transactions was mostly through China's own cross-border payments, while among third-party markets, the usage of RMB is limited. According to China's State Administration of Foreign Exchange (SAFE), in March 2023, the RMB surpassed the USD for the first time for use in China's own cross-border payments. The internationalisation of the RMB is mostly driven by economic policies – the bilateral swap agreements with foreign countries' central banks and the establishment of off-shore RMB clearing centres help facilitate the increased cross-border use of the RMB.[2]

Some studies indicate that trade relations with China and loans (received from China) are the main drivers of cross-border RMB payments, but only for countries in the Belt and Road Initiative (BRI).[3] For non-BRI countries, the swap lines with the People's Bank of China and the Qualified Foreign Institutional Investor (QFII) schemes implemented by China's financial regulator help promote the use of the RMB as a currency for cross-border transactions. The internationalisation of the RMB hence does not appear to be a market-driven process but one steered by governmental economic policies.

An international currency is one that is used and held beyond the borders of the issuing country, not merely for transactions with that country's residents but also, and importantly, for transactions among non-residents. It is one that is widely used to invoice international trade in goods and services (a unit of account); settle payments in trade and financial transactions (a medium of exchange); and denominate financial assets and serve as reserves for foreign central banks (a store of value).[4]

The RMB has made progress in functioning as a "medium of exchange" in global markets. However, there is limited progress as a "store of value" and "unit of account". China accounted for a mere 2.2% of global foreign exchange reserves, whereas the US share was 57.8%, as of 2024 (Figure 3.5). As a unit of account, the dollar is the invoicing currency for 40% of global exports while the euro accounts for another 40% of the world total.[5] By comparison, the RMB's share of global invoicing is very low. Data on other countries including China as a unit of account is fragmentary, but China's global network of currency swap lines has been associated with increases in RMB invoicing, at least in countries for which China accounts for a large share of trade.[6]

Latest available data shows that as of April 2025, China accounted for nearly 9% of turnover in the foreign exchange market where currencies are traded and currency exposures hedged.[7] By comparison, the US dollar is involved in nearly 90% of global FX transactions, making it the single most traded currency in the FX market.[8] By contrast, the Euro is involved in approximately 29% of global FX transactions.[9] The usage of the RMB in cross-border payments and RMB-denominated debt and reserves remain small in the global context.

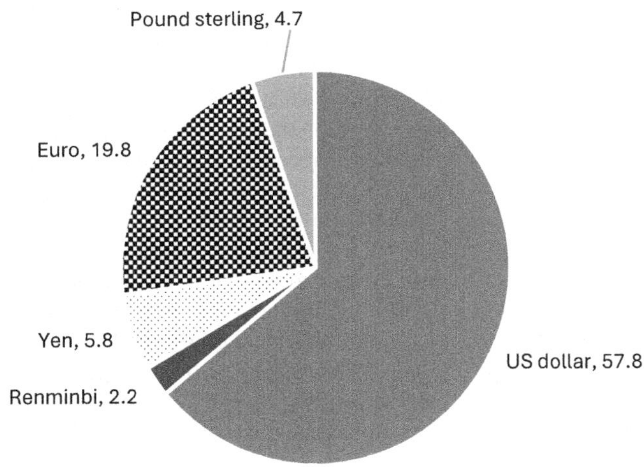

Figure 3.5 World currency composition of official foreign exchange reserves (%), 2024.

Source: COFER, IMF.

Although the share of the RMB in various measures of international use is much lower than the share of China's economy in global trade (20%), past developments suggest that the use of the RMB is gaining momentum in cross-border payment and trade settlement. The use of financial sanctions by the United States following the Russia-Ukraine conflict in 2022 and the "weaponisation" of the dollar have driven many countries to contemplate reducing their dependence on the US currency. Amongst the BRIC countries, Brazil and China reached a deal in April 2023 to trade in their own currencies while Brazil's first RMB-clearing bank was authorised by the People's Bank of China in February 2023 to settle cross-border RMB payments.[10]

Notably, Russia's usage of RMB in trading with China has increased significantly since 2014 when the United States imposed strict sanctions on Russia after the latter's occupation of Crimea. While the central bank of Russia does not release data on RMB settlements specifically, Russia's imports from China settled using RMB are estimated to have risen to 26.8% in 2021 from 2.2% in 2013.[11] For export settlements, the RMB was used to settle 16% of total Russian exports (2022).[12] However, trade between Russia and China accounts for only 27% of the increase in trade settlement in RMB.[13] The remaining 70% is likely RMB-denominated trade in Asia and further abroad in countries such as Argentina and Brazil.[14]

Russian companies are also increasingly using RMB debt financing; Chinese banks' exposure to Russian banks reportedly close to quadrupled when the big four state-owned banks increased their lending to Russia from US$2.2 billion to US$9.7 billion between January 2022 to March 2023.[15] In a bid to move away from the dollar, the Russian Ministry of Finance reportedly said in December 2022 that the Russian National Wealth Fund (sovereign wealth fund) would no longer hold dollar assets while yuan holdings would be allowed to rise to 60% of assets from a previous maximum of 30%.[16]

RMB internationalisation has also benefitted from elevated US interest rates since 2022. Given the higher costs of borrowing in dollars, many borrowers have turned to the RMB for financing or refinancing. For the first time in nearly 20 years, it is substantially cheaper to conduct short-term borrowing in RMB rather than dollars. As a result of the US Federal Reserve's rate hike campaign since March 2022 to rein in inflation, short-term borrowing costs (proxied by the yield of a one-year government bond) in USD had risen considerably from around 1.3 percentage points in March 2022 to 4.84 percentage points in January 2024, around 3.5 percentage points higher than that of the China government bond of the same maturity on average (Figure 3.6). As a result of higher US dollar financing costs, most Chinese companies' offshore financing denominated in dollars has declined since mid-2022; in the first 10 months of 2022, the

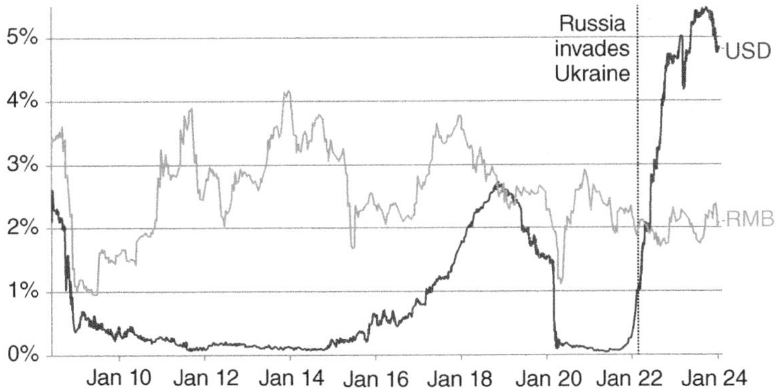

Figure 3.6 Short-term borrowing costs: USD versus RMB (US and China one-year government bill yields).

Source: Bloomberg Finance LLP.

dollar bond issuance of Chinese enterprises decreased by 55% y-o-y while the offshore "dim sum" bond issuance increased.[17]

The use of RMB also appeared to gain impetus due to dollar shortages arising from the US Fed's interest rate hikes. For developing economies, the RMB offers an alternative option to the dollar in trade settlements when there is a dollar liquidity crunch which would have significant spill-overs to domestic funding conditions. Argentina (the third largest economy in Latin America) announced in April 2023 that it will start to pay for Chinese imports in yuan rather than in dollars, given its dwindling FX exchange reserves and shrinking dollar liquidity as a result of the US Fed Reserve's monetary tightening in 2022. It also reportedly reached an agreement with the People's Bank of China to secure US$1.7 billion in yuan through currency swaps to meet its US$2.7 billion payment obligations to the IMF.[18]

The rate differential between the United States and China is enabling some borrowers to lock in a relatively favourable repayment cost. In October 2025, Kenya converted its dollar-denominated railway loans from China into yuan to reduce the debt-servicing cost, although the conversion alone might overlook the risk of yuan appreciation. Ethiopia, a member of BRIC nations, is reportedly also looking to convert at least part of the US$5.38 billion owed to China into yuan-denominated loans.[19] This helps to align with the broader goal of enlarging the global footprint of the yuan. Moreover, as China's policy banks sell yuan bonds at a cost that is much cheaper than issuing dollar debt and the repayment is in yuan, this limits net interest losses to the banks in converting the loans. It is estimated that approximately US$67 billion in outstanding debt is owed to China by the world's poorest countries[20] and if China refinances this debt for longer tenure and lower interest rates, it would benefit the indebted countries while promoting the use of the yuan in financing.

De-dollarisation and Geopolitics

Over the past decade, many countries, primarily emerging economies, have endeavoured to reduce their reliance on the US dollar in global payment transactions. Some of the push for de-dollarisation is in reaction to the United States' "weaponisation" of the dollar, particularly following Russia's invasion of Ukraine. Concerns about dollar hegemony have also grown more acute in response to monetary tightening in the United States which led to high interest rates and a recent dollar glut. Rapidly rising interest rates in the United States have, broadly speaking, attracted capital away from developing economies and strengthened the dollar relative to emerging market currencies. This is further exacerbated by the Russia-Ukraine war's spillover effects on food and energy prices, resulting in the surging cost of importing dollar-priced commodities in emerging markets.

Developing countries, particularly those with weak economic fundamentals, are susceptible to the impact arising from vulnerabilities to the US dollar. A strong US dollar has further compounded the worsening macroeconomic situation of Argentina, for instance, which faces persistent budget deficits and also risks of currency mismatches that have arisen from high external debt denominated in US dollar. In October 2023, Argentina's inflation rate was a staggering 143%, Egypt's was 36% while that in Ethiopia was 29%.[21]

These macro headwinds have supported de-dollarisation efforts. Rising dollar borrowing costs and declining dollar liquidity inadvertently push firms to adopt the RMB for their trade financing needs. Unlike developed economies which had readily available dollar supply through the swap line arrangements with the US Federal Reserve, most emerging market economies had much less access to dollar funding, notably those without access to the swap lines. Further, concerned about vulnerabilities to potential financial sanctions as a result of the dependence on the dollar and the Western-centric payment infrastructure for global transactions, developing economies have started to embrace the RMB.

Initiatives to increase the RMB's use are evident in South Africa, Egypt and Saudi Arabia. In May 2022, a China-Africa cross-border settlement centre in Zhejiang province was established to facilitate direct RMB cross-border payments. As is the case, more than 5% of Cameroon, Kenya and Tanzania's external debt is denominated in RMB.[22] In October 2023, Egypt (a new member of BRICS) was the first African economy to issue a Panda bond (approximately US$500 million worth of RMB-denominated debt with a large Chinese state-owned bank acting as the lead underwriter) to finance green and social projects.[23]

Chinese and Saudi central banks were reported to have established a bilateral swap line, following high-level Chinese-Saudi discussions aimed at facilitating China's RMB-invoiced petrol trade with Saudi Arabia, which reportedly exports approximately 25% of its oil to China. However, there does not seem to be a significant increase in the share of oil transactions in RMB which is somewhat surprising as China is the world's largest oil importer and has specific arrangements for RMB settlements with major exporters (from Russia to Saudi Arabia).[24] The share of the global oil trade priced in dollars remains around 80%, despite China's recent efforts to promote the renminbi.[25]

In a strategic move to reduce its reliance on the dollar particularly in commodity markets, the Shanghai Gold Exchange (SGE) launched its first offshore vault in Hong Kong along with the rollout of two new yuan-denominated gold contracts in June 2025. By positioning itself as a custodian for foreign sovereign gold reserves through the SGE, China hopes to encourage partner nations to buy and store gold in custodian warehouses linked to the SGE's International Board, which was launched in 2014 to allow foreign and domestic holders of offshore yuan to trade physical gold. China's bid to hold foreign gold reserves and its increased purchases of gold have been interpreted by market analysts as incremental de-dollarisation.[26] According to the World Gold Council, gold accounted for 7% of China's total foreign exchange reserves in August 2025, up from around 3% in late 2022,[27] fuelled by geopolitical conflicts that are exacerbated by the US-China trade war, economic uncertainty, a weakening US dollar and diversification away from the US dollar towards gold as the "ultimate safe-haven asset".

US Dollar Dominance

When it comes to its share of global trade finance, RMB usage has made great strides, even though it is nowhere near challenging the dollar's prevalence. It still lags far behind the dollar as a form of foreign reserves,[28] an invoicing currency for trade, a store of value for non-resident investors and a unit for use in hedging currency exposure. It has yet to be a fully functioning safe haven asset in terms of its ability to hedge or counter financial market volatility.[29] There is less liquidity to trade the Chinese yuan compared to the US dollar, which enjoys a more liquid market that makes hedging the US dollar less costly and risky.

In addition, currency pairs involving the dollar are generally more liquid and thus less costly to exchange than emerging market currency pairs. The dollar is therefore oftentimes used to facilitate exchanges between emerging market currencies.[30] As a result, even when cross-border trade is invoiced in a local currency, the dollar may ultimately play a role in facilitating that transaction. The fact that many BRI loans are in US dollars attests to the fact that it is low-cost, less risky and more convenient for both the Chinese lender and overseas borrower to use US dollars instead of the RMB.

The frequent usage of the dollar in trade reinforces its use in finance. The large volume of US dollar invoiced in international trade creates an increased demand for US dollar deposits, giving the US dollar a disproportionate advantage in reducing borrowing costs.[31] The dominance of the dollar is sustained by complementarities between the different functions of an international currency – firms typically borrow in the same currency in which they invoice their exports and receive payments, and central banks tend to keep as foreign reserves the same currency that domestic banks and firms use for trade settlement and financial transaction. This further solidifies the US dollar's position as a global currency.[32]

Given that the US dollar continues to be the dominant currency in the world, it appears that alternative payment systems like the Cross-Border Interbank Payments System (CIPS)[33] would pose no imminent threat to SWIFT and of supplanting the US-dominated global financial system. CIPS was established in 2015 as part of China's efforts in building the infrastructure to support the RMB as a currency for global payments. It was designed to streamline and enhance cross-border payments and allowed global banks to clear cross-border RMB transactions directly onshore, instead of through clearing banks in offshore RMB hubs. Transactions by CIPS are reported to be growing rapidly; average daily CIPS transactions reportedly increased by 50% in 2022 after Russia invaded Ukraine,[34] and by about another 25% in the first three quarters of 2023.[35] There could be greater usage of CIPS down the road (and by extension, accelerate the internationalisation of the RMB) if more countries, aiming to wean their dependence on the US dollar, turn to CIPS, which is evolving as a core component of global payment infrastructure. However, it may be hard for CIPS to become a viable substitute to the SWIFT network in the near future, especially since most of China's CIPS transactions still use the SWIFT network.[36]

Pre-requisites for RMB Internationalisation

One argument suggests that the RMB can be an international and reserve currency only if China runs current account deficits, as does the United States. Only by importing more than it exports to the rest of the world will China be able to supply adequate quantities of its currency for use by non-Chinese residents. As noted by Prasad and Ye (2012),[37] this argument overgeneralises – while the United States and the United Kingdom run chronic current account deficits, the same is not true for the Eurozone or Japan, whose currencies are also used internationally. Consequently, it is not essential for a country to run persistent current account deficits in order to attain reserve currency status. This is related to the Triffin Dilemma, in that the reserve currency-issuing country cannot possibly ensure an adequate supply of its currency for use in the international monetary system without undermining the stability of the currency.

In effect, international reserve currencies are supplied primarily through the capital and financial account, instead of the current account.[38] The reserve currency country not only provides liquidity by issuing short-term liabilities that non-residents would use for international trade and investment, but also invests in other countries and runs net foreign asset positions. Hence, lending to and making claims on non-residents by Chinese financial institutions and firms would be the main source of creating RMB liquidity in the international monetary system.[39]

The implication from the Triffin Dilemma has generated a lot of debate, with the former People's Bank of China Governor Zhou Xiaochuan pointing out that to overcome the difficulties in the international monetary system arising from the Dilemma, it is necessary to create a super-sovereign international reserve currency in the long term.[40] As an interim step in the medium term, it is necessary to diversify the currency composition of international reserves and from the issuers of such currencies. The internationalisation of the RMB can be seen as a part of this effort.

As part of its efforts to facilitate more use of the RMB, China is likely to continue to invest in the infrastructure for RMB payments, establish additional official offshore RMB clearing banks and extend additional bilateral RMB swaps with foreign central banks. These bilateral swap lines enable central banks in foreign countries to access RMB liquidity without relying on the US dollar. Since the 2008 global financial crisis, the People's Bank of China has signed bilateral swap agreements with 32 countries totalling nearly 4.5 trillion yuan.[41] A new International Monetary Fund study (2023) found that bilateral swap agreements have played a positive role in facilitating the use of RMB in cross-border settlement. However, it remains to be seen if the use of such tools will facilitate increased use of the RMB in cross-border payments, given the inconvertibility of the capital account. The delay in the opening of the capital account would slow down the pace of RMB internationalisation.

To facilitate capital market opening and by extension RMB internationalisation, reforms of China's financial system are imperative as it is still characterised by financial repression. The banking sector is based on interest rates controls, dominance of state-owned banks, entry barriers and control of credit allocation in preference of state-owned enterprises.

Although there was a reform in 2019 to make the lending rates more market-driven – by requiring all loans to reference the more market-driven Loan Prime Rate instead of the benchmark lending rate (which is not responsive to market conditions) – interest rates are still, to a large extent, not market-determined.[42]

Further, the development of the bond market is crucial for the healthy development of the capital market, which in turn is necessary for the RMB to become a truly global currency. China's bond market faces significant challenges, including regulatory fragmentation, moral hazard, a relatively narrow investor base and low foreign ownership (by international standards, the scale of the Chinese bond market is disproportionately small).[43] A broad, deep and liquid bond market is crucial to make the RMB more attractive as a store of value for foreigners when they can freely invest in China's bond market.

In addition, a weak institutional framework is an impediment to China's RMB internationalisation. In order for the RMB to be a "safe-haven currency", trust in China's institutions like rule of law, an independent judiciary and enforcement of contracts is important. Credibility of the government is equally vital as China is governed by a one-party state that has a different ideology from essentially all of the Western developed countries. China's territorial claims in the South China Sea, for instance, has been criticised as being completely illegitimate. It would be difficult for a country's currency to gain worldwide acceptance if there is no trust in the government and the currency it issues.

Prospects for RMB Internationalisation

China has more motivations than other countries, such as Japan, to internationalise its currency. Due to its ideological differences with the United States, China has a strong desire to be more independent from the United States and the dollar compared to countries like Japan, which is an ally of the United States. Further, being able to borrow internationally in China's own currency is an important benefit as borrowing in one's own currency would reduce the risk of currency mismatch (i.e. differences in the currencies in which assets and liabilities are denominated).[44] In addition, when a currency is widely used as a settlement and funding currency, the country's citizens and government might be able to borrow large amounts abroad at low interest rates in the country's own currency.

When the RMB becomes sufficiently internationalised, there would be more flexibility in the exchange rate (Impossible Trinity) and the exchange rate with the USD can fluctuate more than before without causing instability in the financial system. Since China does not need to intervene as much as before to stabilise the RMB exchange rate against the USD, it will not need to accumulate as much low-interest bearing dollar-denominated assets such as US Treasury bonds as before. In this sense, it can decouple itself from the "dollar trap".[45]

China's ambition to internationalise its RMB may well be bolstered by its central bank digital currency (CBDC). It is leading the way among major economies in trialling the CBDC and involved in the Multiple Central Bank Digital Currency (m-CBDC) Bridge project with Hong Kong, Thailand and the United Arab Emirates to explore the cross-border use of the digital currencies in payments and settlement of both international trade and capital market transactions. If the m-CBDC network is developed, or China helps other nations to develop their own CBDCs to be interoperable with the e-CNY, this may help expedite efforts to internationalise the RMB. Once the central banks of countries use digital currencies in direct settlement arrangements with each other rather than go through the dollar, which is currently used as an intermediating currency in most trade and financial transactions, it may facilitate greater usage of the RMB. It may also spur the increasing adoption of the CIPS as an international payment system.

Thus far, it appears that the CBDC has yet to become a game changer. China's e-CNY still struggles with widespread domestic adoption due to competition from domestic payment giants like Alipay and WeChat Pay. Cross-border payments also encounter issues – such as monetary sovereignty and regulatory requirements – and raise challenges for monetary authorities in managing cross-border capital flows. Encouraging foreign users to adopt a new digital currency is even more challenging because such a decision goes beyond economic rationales to factors such as trust and data protection. At the moment, the CBDC is designed mainly for domestic retail payments. However, that may change, and the e-CNY could be used in a hypothetical scenario whereby a Chinese company faces the threat of being unable to send money overseas if it is sanctioned by the West and barred from SWIFT.

China's central bank digital currency can facilitate the ease of adoption of RMB even though the structural factors determining the widespread usage of the currency are still capital account convertibility. It will not have a significant impact on the status of the US dollar as a reserve and safe haven currency. Of late, China has reportedly been mulling the development of a yuan-backed stablecoin – a type of cryptocurrency designed to maintain a stable value by being pegged to a reference asset, typically a fiat currency or in some cases, commodities like gold – as part of its strategy to enhance the global influence of the RMB and counter the dominance of the US dollar. China's consideration of stablecoins, with pilot programmes in Hong Kong and Shanghai, is motivated by the widespread use of the US dollar-backed stablecoin; if adoption of the USD-backed stablecoins increases, issuers will need to hold more US dollar or dollar-denominated assets to support the peg and this enables stealth dollarisation and entrench the position of the US dollar as the dominant reserve currency. This presents a dilemma for China whose goal is to reduce reliance on US-dominated financial systems. Additionally, there is also the challenge of ensuring regulatory compliance given concerns about transparency and surveillance. In short, while technological innovations could accelerate de-dollarisation with CBDCs (blockchain technology) and decentralised finance providing mechanisms to bypass traditional dollar-based financial systems, they are not without challenges. The current consensus is that the RMB would not dethrone or displace the US dollar anytime soon.

Notes

1 Natixis RMB Internationalization Monitor.

2 Song and Xia, "Bilateral swap agreements and renminbi settlement in cross-border trade", *Economic and Political Studies*, 8(3), July 2020; Bahaj and Reis, "Jumpstarting an international currency", Bank of England Working Paper No. 874, 2020; Zucker-Marques et al., "The role of institutions: A cross-country analysis of renminbi trading in foreign exchange markets", *China and World Economy*, 30(3), 2022.

3 Alessia Amighini and Alicia García-Herrero, "Third time lucky? China's push to internationalise the renminbi", *Policy Brief*, 20/2023, Bruegel, 2023.

4 An international currency should fulfil three functions – *medium of exchange* (i.e. used in direct exchange of currencies and as a vehicle currency in carrying out indirect exchanges between two other currencies in foreign trade and international capital transactions); *unit of account* (used by private agents to invoice merchandise trade, to denominate financial transactions, and by official agents to define exchange rate parities); *store of value* (i.e. held either as bonds by non-residents or financial assets denominated in it as reserve assets).

5 Boz, Ermine, Camila Casas, Georgios Georgiadis, Gita Gopinath, Helena le Mezo, Arnaud Mehl and Tra Nguyen, "Patterns in invoicing currency in global trade", IMF Working Paper, no. 20/126, 2022.

6 Georgios Georgiadis, Helena Le Mezo, Arnaud Mehl, Cédric Tille, "Fundamentals vs policies: can the US dollar's dominance in global trade be dented?" ECB Working Paper series no. 2574, July 2021.

7 BIS Triennial Central Bank Survey 2025.

8 BIS Triennial Central Bank Survey 2025.

9 BIS Triennial Central Bank Survey 2025.

10 "ICBC Brazil processes First RMB settlement transaction", *China Daily*, 12 April 2023.

11 Since 2020, countries with the largest share of official foreign exchange reserves in RMB have included Russia (17%) and Tanzania (16%). Goldman Sachs, "Progress Check on RMB Internationalization", 2 July 2023. https://www.gspublishing.com/content/research/en/reports/

2023/07/02/450c00ac-c2ae-4a96-a5e5-26534e7e493c.html (accessed 26 February 2024).
12 "Russia embraces China's renminbi in face of Western sanctions", *Financial Times*, 25 March 2023.
13 Niels Graham and Hung Tran, "Dedollarization is not just geopolitics, economic fundamentals matter", January 2024. https://www.atlanticcouncil.org/blogs/econographics/dedollarization-is-not-just-geopolitics-economic-fundamentals-matter/ (accessed 29 February 2024).
14 Niels Graham and Hung Tran, "Dedollarization is not just geopolitics, economic fundamentals matter", January 2024. https://www.atlanticcouncil.org/blogs/econographics/dedollarization-is-not-just-geopolitics-economic-fundamentals-matter/ (accessed 29 February 2024).
15 "Chinese lenders extend billions of dollars to Russian banks after western sanctions", *Financial Times*, 4 September 2023.
16 At the time of the announcement, the fund held 310 billion yuan ($45.5 billion) worth of assets denominated in the Chinese currency. "Russia's embrace of yuan cannot bring financial stability", *Nikkei Asia*, 14 February 2023. https://asia.nikkei.com/opinion/russia-s-embrace-of-yuan-cannot-bring-financial-stability (accessed 26 February 2024).
17 HKTDC, "RMB Internationalization Standing at an Important Breaking Point in 2023", 20 January 2023.
18 "Argentina strikes deal with People's Bank of China to secure US$1.7 billion in yuan for IMF debt", *South China Morning Post*, 1 August 2023.
19 "China finds costly new way of boosting Xi's global yuan push", *Bloomberg*, 24 October 2025.
20 "China finds costly new way of boosting Xi's global yuan push", *Bloomberg*, 24 October 2025.
21 Valentina Romei and Alan Smith, "Global inflation tracker: See how your country compares on rising prices", *Financial Times*, 30 November 2023, https://www.ft.com/content/088d3368-bb8b-4ff3-9df7-a7680d4d81b2.
22 Chi Lo, "The renminbi's creeping internationalisation (IV): BRICS expansion and the rise of Africa", 27 September 2023. https://viewpoint.bnpparibas-am.com/the-renminbis-creeping-internationalisation-iv-brics-expansion-and-the-rise-of-africa.
23 "Egypt Issues Africa's First Sustainable Panda Bond Worth 3.5 billion RMB Backed by African Development Bank and Asian Infrastructure Investment Bank", African Development Bank Group, 17 October 2023. https://www.afdb.org/en/news-and-events/press-releases/egypt-issues-africas-first-sustainable-panda-bond-worth-35-billion-rmb-backed-african-development-bank-and-asian-infrastructure-investment-bank-65097.
24 Refer to source in Endnote 3.
25 Kenneth Rogoff, *Our Dollar, Your Problem: An Insider's View of Seven Turbulent Decades of Global Finance, and the Road Ahead*. Yale University Press, 2025.

26 "China courts foreign gold reserves to boost global clout", *Bloomberg*, 23 September 2025.

27 "China gold market update: Wholesale demand fell in August", *World Gold Council*, 16 September 2025.

28 Foreign exchange reserves to facilitate the servicing of the country's foreign currency liabilities are typically in US dollar. In 2022, approximately 58% of disclosed global foreign exchange reserves were dollar assets. Robert Greene, "The difficult realities of the BRICS' dedollarization efforts – and the renminbi's role", *Carnegie Endowment for International Peace*, 5 December 2023.

29 Xin Cheng, Hongyi Chen, and Yinggang Zhou, "Is the renminbi a safe-haven currency? Evidence from conditional coskewness and cokurtosis", *Journal of International Money and Finance*, 113, May 2021.

30 Recent research indicates that roughly 40% of foreign exchange turnover for the dollar is driven by its use to facilitate the exchange of two other currencies. Fabricius Somogyi, "Dollar dominance in FX trading", Northeastern University D'Amore-McKim School of Business research paper No. 4067388, 9 September 2023, https://papers.ssrn.com/sol3/papers.cfm?abstract_id=3882546 (accessed 29 February 2024).

31 If a currency is an invoicing currency for the trade of certain goods in a foreign country, it is usually also a settlement currency for the goods in that country. There will be demand for liquidity in that currency, which induces market participants to own bank deposits (store of value).

32 Gita Gopinath and Jeremy Stein, "Banking, trade and the making of a dominant currency", *The Quarterly Journal of Economics* 136, 2021. In the study highlighting the fundamental connection between the US dollar as the primary currency for invoicing by non-US exporters and its prominent position in the global banking and financial industry, the authors argue that the US dollar can still maintain its dominant position in the medium term even in the face of rapid global export growth in other economies such as Europe and China. However, they added that in the long run, "if the gap between the US and these economies widens to a certain extent, the US dollar could fall from the world stage, as what happened with the British pound in the early 20th century".

33 SWIFT and CIPS provide secure data transmission for banks that clear customer payments. However, CIPS still depends on SWIFT for international financial messaging and its messaging system is still not as efficient as SWIFT which has participation from an estimated 11,000 banks.

34 Haruki Kitagawa and Akira Inujima, "Russia speeds shift to ruble and yuan as sanctions bite", *Nikkei Asia*, 23 February 2023, https://asia.nikkei.com/Business/Markets/Currencies/Russia-speeds-shift-to-ruble-and-yuan-as-sanctions-bite (accessed 29 February 2024).

35 About 21,000 average daily CIPS transactions were reported in January 2023 and about 26,500 average daily CIPS transactions were reported in September 2023. See "Homepage", Cross-Border Interbank Payments System, https://www.cips.com.cn/en/index/index.html.

36 CIPS started with 19 direct participants and 176 indirect participants from 50 countries; at the end of January 2022, there were 1,280 participants from 103 countries. Marco Cipriani, Linda Goldberg and Gabriele La Spada, "Financial Sanctions, SWIFT, and the Architecture of the International Payments System", New York Fed Staff Report, no. 1047, January 2023.

37 Eswar Prasad and Lei (Sandy) Ye, "The renminbi's role in the global monetary system", *Brookings*, February 2012.

38 Dong He, "'The triffin dilemma' and currency internationalisation", *Caijing Magazine*, 3 December 2012.

39 According to Prasad, the reserve currency economies have diverse net international positions. The United States had a particularly large negative net foreign asset position, amounting to $2.5 trillion in 2010. Germany, Japan and Switzerland have net asset positions, with Japan's position in particular being a massive $3.1 trillion. The United Kingdom and also the euro area as a whole have negative net asset positions. This diversity suggests that the signs of the net positions are themselves not crucial for reserve currency status. In other words, it is not essential for a country to run persistent current account deficits, as suggested by the Triffin Dilemma, for its currency to attain reserve currency status.

40 Refer to source in Endnote 38.

41 Caixin Global, "Cover story: How the yuan is taking over the dollar's role in global trade", 8 September 2025.

42 This is despite the scrapping of all lending rate ceiling and floors by 2013 and the removal of the cap on deposit rates in 2015. There are still hidden interest-rate controls, with the benchmark interest rates and administrative directives still distorting capital allocation.

43 Edwin L-C Lai, *One Currency, Two Markets: China's Attempt to Internationalize the Renminbi*. Cambridge University Press, June 2021.

44 Barry Eichengreen and Ricardo Hausmann (1999) call the phenomenon that a less developed country cannot borrow in its own currency "original sin". It was this "original sin" that led to currency mismatches between the revenues and debts of the firms in countries such as Thailand and Indonesia during the 1997–1998 Asian Financial Crisis. If Chinese citizens can mostly borrow internationally in their own currency, they can avoid the "original sin" problem.

Eichengreen, Barry, Hausmann, Ricardo and Panizza, Ugo, "Currency mismatches, debt intolerance and original sin: Why they are not the same and why it matters", NBER Working Paper 10036, October 2003.

45 Refer to source in Endnote 43.

4 Geopolitics and Global Value Chain in East Asia (I)

The Case of the Semiconductor Industry

Global Interdependencies along the Semiconductor Supply Chain

The semiconductor industry is a highly globalised, complex and specialised sector, with an interconnected network of geographically diverse companies that engaged in design, manufacturing and assembly. Characterised by deep specialisation and labour division, regions or countries focus on distinct areas or processes (e.g. design, fabrication, assembly), or technologies (e.g. memory chips, processors). As such, only a few market leaders dominate in the different segments of the semiconductor global value chains, from design software and intellectual property to materials and equipment suppliers.

US-headquartered companies, for instance, specialise in the fabless chip design segment while relying on Taiwanese and South Korean foundries to manufacture their chips. The foundries themselves rely on equipment, chemicals and silicon wafers from the United States, Europe and Japan. The semiconductor front-end (wafer fabrication) and back-end (ATP or assembling, testing and packaging[1]) activities are largely concentrated in East Asia chiefly in China, Taiwan, South Korea and Japan. Southeast Asia is home to significant ATP activity, accounting for approximately 20% of total global ATP capacity,[2] with Malaysia capturing the greatest share within the region.[3] In fact, Southeast Asia ranks third after China (31%) and Taiwan (21%) in back-end processes.[4] In recent years, alongside the increasingly mature semiconductor manufacturing clusters in ASEAN countries, semiconductor equipment manufacturers have also been expanding their presence in the region, particularly in Singapore, Malaysia or the Philippines. These companies are mainly from the United States, Europe and Japan (such as Applied Materials, ASML and Tokyo Electron). The production of semiconductors is thus very integrated, globalised and at the same time extremely specialised.

The sophisticated processes of chip design and production and their concomitant ecosystems of highly specialised firms imply that no single

DOI: 10.4324/9781003674221-4

economy can be self-sufficient in the entire semiconductor value chain.[5] Recognising the semiconductor industry's strategic importance from national security, the United States, China and Europe have launched sweeping industrial policies, including huge state subsidies to generous tax and financial incentives, aimed at bolstering their domestic semiconductor capabilities.

As semiconductors grow increasingly critical to powering artificial intelligence, the industry has emerged as a key geopolitical tool for countries to extend their influence and out compete other rival countries. The global semiconductor industry has become a focal point of geopolitical tension, with semiconductors currently at the centre of the escalating trade tensions and intensifying technological rivalry between the United States and China.

The semiconductor industry thus provides a useful case study to examine how geopolitical changes have resulted in shifts in trade flows within the global supply chain. This is particularly so since semiconductors are strategically important for Asian economies as significant players in the global semiconductor supply chain.

Mapping the Semiconductor Ecosystem

The semiconductor supply chain in this analysis is classified using OECD (2019) product definitions[6] (see Appendix 4.1 for HS codes). Its production process takes place in four stages: (i) raw materials (specialty chemicals, silicon carbide, germanium) and other semiconductor materials are processed to form silicon wafers (the output of Step 1 in Figure 4.1); (ii) with additional inputs and equipment, wafers are converted into semiconductors in Step 2 of Figure 4.1; (iii) the semiconductors or integrated circuits are further processed with other electrical apparatus (inputs like diodes and transistors) to form intermediate electronic goods (Step 3 in Figure 4.1); and (iv) the intermediate parts are incorporated or assembled into final (or finished) products for industrial (for instance, data processing machines) or consumer use (for example, smartphones) (Output 1 and 2 in Step 4, Figure 4.1).

Semiconductor production involves a highly geographically fragmented value chain with complex international linkages. Using granular trade data from the UN Comtrade database to track the semiconductor production process, different countries lead different segments of the supply chain. In general, the EU, Japan and the United States are more involved in the upstream segments of the supply chain, while Taiwan and South Korea are in the middle segment of the supply chain and China is at the middle and downstream stages.

In the initial stage (Step 1, Figure 4.1), an examination of the trade balance of raw materials required for wafer production reveals that China

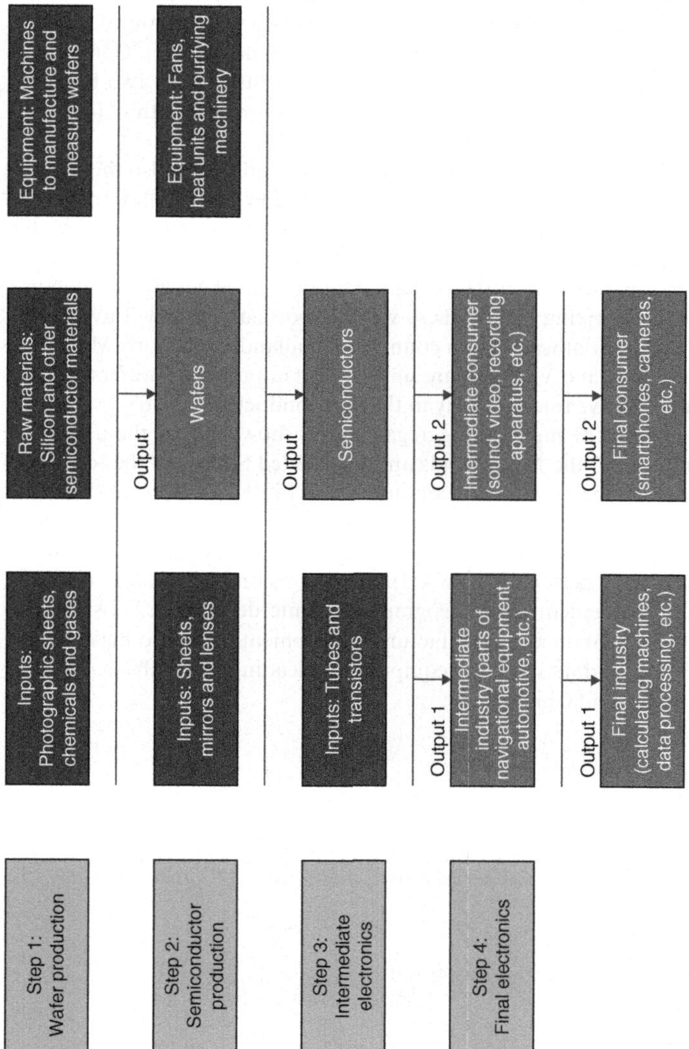

Figure 4.1 Supply chain of semiconductors in traded goods.

Source: OECD 2019.

is the largest net importer of raw inputs in 2023 followed by other East Asian and Southeast Asian economies such as Japan, Korea, Taiwan, Singapore and Thailand. Although China is one of the world's major purified industrial silicon producers, it is still the largest net importer of high-purity silicon.[7] The United States exports a large share of silicon, with Hemlock as one of its largest polysilicon manufacturers. Germany is also a top exporter of high-purity silicon, accounting for two-fifths of global high-purity silicon exports in 2024, with more than a third (44%) of these exports going to China.[8]

The top net importers of raw materials are incidentally also the top net exporters of wafers, reflecting the fact that China and Japan import raw materials for the production of wafers. While China and Japan are the leading net importers of raw materials for wafer production, they are also the top net exporters of wafers essential for integrated circuit manufacturing. At the receiving end of these wafer exports are mostly Taiwan and South Korea. Southeast Asian countries (Thailand, Singapore, Malaysia, the Philippines and Vietnam) are similarly net importers of wafers, underscoring the active role they play in the semiconductor industry.

An analysis of highly disaggregated data shows that in the upstream segment, Japan, the Netherlands and the United States are the top three exporters of specialised semiconductor machinery in chips and wafers manufacturing (HS code 848620). Combined, they accounted for two-thirds (68.3%) of the world's exports of specialised chip machinery during the 2021–2023 period (Figure 4.2).[9] The semiconductor value chain is both highly fragmented and geographically interdependent. Fabs depend on these semiconductor manufacturing equipment (SME) to make chips, while SME vendors sell these equipment to leading-edge fabs in Taiwan, South Korea and China.[10]

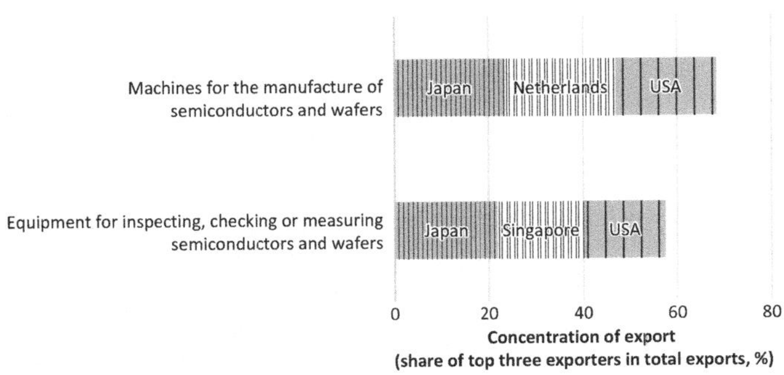

Figure 4.2 Share of top three exporters in total exports (2021–2023), %.

Source: UN Comtrade.

The latest trade data show that in 2023, the Asian economies of China, South Korea, Taiwan, Singapore and Malaysia accounted for more than half or 60% of global chip exports. China, Taiwan and South Korea accounted for a combined export share of 42% or two-fifths of global chip exports. In contrast, the United States and Japan constituted only 8% of global chip exports in the same year. While the semiconductor exports are dominated by the Northeast Asian economies of Taiwan, China and South Korea, export leadership varies substantially across various chip types. Taiwan and China are the top two exporters in all integrated circuit (IC) types except for memory chips, where Korea is leading.

The semiconductors, according to the OECD, can be separated into two broad categories – ICs and discrete as well as other chips like opto-electronics and sensors. Chips or ICs, a subset of semiconductors, mainly take the form of memory, logic, micro (processors) or analogue circuits. Taiwan has the largest trade balance in electronic integrated circuits (HS code 8542); its net exports of chips amounted to around US$186 billion in 2023, whereas South Korea hit US$69 billion. Taiwan and South Korea hold strong positions in semiconductor manufacturing, with Taiwan capturing over 70% of advanced node (less than 10 nanometres) chip manufacturing.[11] China, on the other hand, is a net importer of ICs (HS 8542), registering a deficit of US$214 billion in 2023.

The final product in which semiconductors are integrated (Step 4 output in Figure 4.1) can be separated into final goods for consumers and final goods for industry. China has the largest share of exports for both categories; as of the latest available data from UN Comtrade, in 2023, China accounted for approximately 32% of the world's final (or finished) goods destined for both industrial and consumer use.

Restructuring and the Changing Landscape

The semiconductor industry has been the focal point of the escalating US-China trade war and the heightened geopolitical tensions. Since 2018, the United States has progressively tightened restrictions on China's access to advanced semiconductor technology. Apart from increased tariffs on China's goods, including semiconductors, export controls were further expanded in 2020 to prevent Chinese companies from acquiring chips made with US technology, even if manufactured overseas. New export controls were further imposed by the United States in October 2024 on semiconductor manufacturing equipment and software tools, further curbing China's ability to produce advanced chips. In early 2025, the US Commerce Department announced stricter enforcement, threatening significant fines for violations of export restrictions. These policies reflect the United States' long-term strategy of curbing China's semiconductor ambitions and protecting US technological leadership.

After the tariff hike in 2018–2019, the United States has significantly reduced its imports of semiconductor-related products from China. In contrast, its imports from Asian economies such as Vietnam and Taiwan have risen.[12] Figure 4.3 shows that the pace of increase in China's exports since 2018 almost matches that of US imports, until 2022 when signs of decoupling in the trade of tech-related products between the United States and China began to emerge. While the United States has shifted its import sources of downstream semiconductor-related products from China to other Asian economies, China remains connected to the global supply chain by manufacturing and exporting intermediate components to Asian economies, which subsequently ship the finished or final products to the United States. In short, China still plays the role of the world's major supplier of semiconductor-related goods.

The share of exports from China to Vietnam and the ASEAN countries of Singapore, Malaysia, Thailand and the Philippines has surged, especially in the trade of intermediate products such as automotive parts or sound/video recording devices. In 2012, the share of such intermediate electronics rose from 21% to 28% in 2023 (Figure 4.4), while the share of the end users of semiconductors (for instance, in finished electronics goods such as cameras, phones and automatic data processors like calculators) declined by 2 percentage points to 17% in 2023.

Evidently, China has integrated its chip industry with key sectors such as automotive, consumer electronics, industrial manufacturing and AI-driven applications in its quest for self-sufficiency in various facets of the semiconductor industry. Such a strategy increases domestic demand

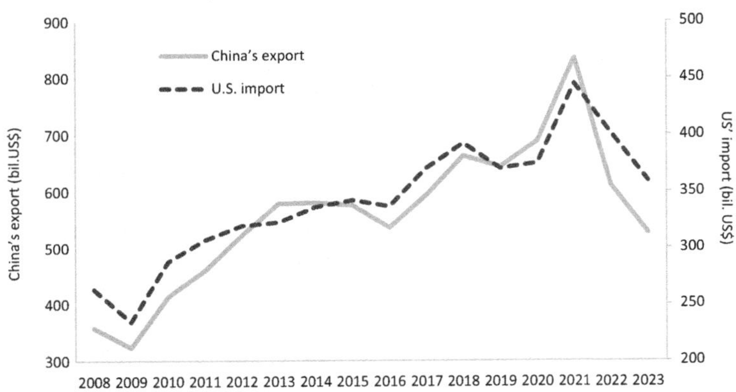

Figure 4.3 Trade in semiconductor-related products, 2008–2023.

Source: UN Comtrade.

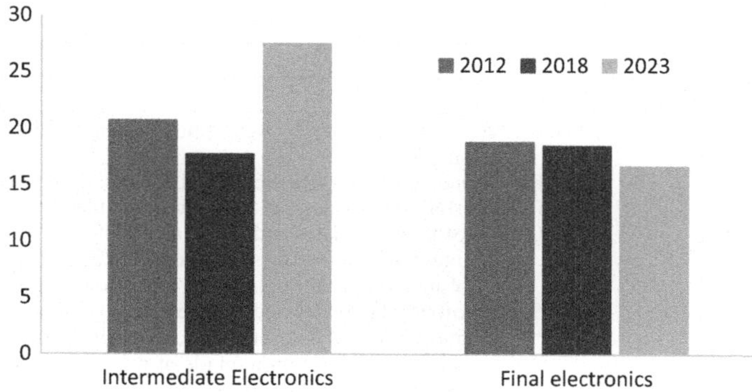

Figure 4.4 China's semiconductor-related exports to ASEAN (%), selected years.

Source: UN Comtrade.

and pushes firms to scale up their processes to ensure cost efficiency and enable large-scale commercialisation of semiconductor-related products.

In the automotive sector, Chinese firms are ramping up in-house production of automotive-grade semiconductors, especially for electric vehicles and autonomous driving. In consumer electronics, domestic chips are increasingly used in smartphones while in industrial automation and manufacturing, China integrates semiconductors into robotics and Internet of Things (IoT) applications, enhancing efficiency and digital transformation. The growing adoption of AI and cloud computing drive the demand for high-performance chips, prompting significant investment in data centres and AI accelerators.[13] This synergistic approach helps to boost semiconductor sales and consolidate China's position as an important player in the global semiconductor market.

As China makes rapid progress in multiple semiconductor domains, the global semiconductor landscape is experiencing a significant realignment, particularly in the midst of geopolitical tensions. US tariffs, export controls and various restrictions on advanced chips and semiconductor manufacturing equipment have accelerated China's pursuit of technological self-reliance. Heightened geopolitical tensions arising from the US-China strategic rivalry risk severely disrupting the highly fragmented semiconductor value chain, with significant repercussions for both upstream suppliers and downstream users. Economies susceptible to the US-China tech war would have to navigate the increasingly complex and fast evolving landscape as superpower confrontation intensifies and global uncertainties continue to mount.

Appendix 4.1 HS codes related to different steps in the semiconductor supply chain

Step 1: Wafer Production		
Raw Materials	*HS Code*	*Description*
	280461	Silicon; containing by weight not less than 99.99% of silicon
	284920	Silicon carbides, whether or not chemically defined
	282560	Germanium oxides and zirconium dioxide
Inputs	370130	Photographic plates and film; flat, sensitised, unexposed, with any side exceeding 225 mm, made of materials other than paper, paperboard or textiles
	370199	Photographic plates and film; (excluding colour photography), flat, sensitised, unexposed, with no side exceeding 255mm, made of materials other than paper, paperboard or textiles
	370790	Photographic goods; chemical preparations (excluding sensitised emulsions), packaged in measured portions or ready-to-use retail form
	811299	Gallium, germanium, indium, niobium (columbium) and vanadium; articles thereof, (excluding unwrought forms, waste, scrap and powders)
Equipment	848610	Machines and apparatus of a kind used solely or principally for the manufacturing of semiconductor boules or wafers
	848690	Machines and apparatus of heading 8486; parts and accessories thereof
	903082	Instruments and apparatus for measuring or checking semiconductor wafers or devices (including integrated circuits)
	903141	Optical instruments and appliances for inspecting semiconductor wafers, devices, photomasks or reticles used in manufacturing semiconductor devices, n.e.c. in chapter 90
Output	381800	Chemical elements doped for use in electronics, in the form of discs, wafers or similar shapes; and chemical compounds doped for use in electronics

Step 2: Semiconductor Production		
Raw Materials	*HS Code*	*Description*
	Output from Step 1	
Inputs	900120	Optical elements; polarising material, sheets and plates thereof
	900190	Optical elements; lenses n.e.c. in heading no. 9001, prisms, mirrors and other optical elements, unmounted, of any material (excluding elements of glass not optically worked)
	900219	Lenses; objective (other than for cameras, projectors or photographic enlargers or reducers), mounted, of any material (excluding elements of glass not optically worked)
	900220	Filters, mounted as parts or fittings for instruments or apparatus, of any material (excluding elements of glass not optically worked)

(*Continued*)

Appendix 4.1 (Continued)

	900290	Optical elements; n.e.c. in heading no. 9002 (e.g. prisms and mirrors), mounted, being parts or fittings for instruments or apparatus, of any material (excluding elements of glass not optically worked)
	901210	Microscopes (excluding optical microscopes); diffraction apparatus
	901290	Microscopes (excluding optical microscopes); diffraction apparatus; parts and accessories thereof
	903082	Instruments and apparatus for measuring or checking semiconductor wafers or devices (including integrated circuits)
	903141	Optical instruments and appliances for inspecting semiconductor wafers or devices or for inspecting photomasks or reticles used in manufacturing semiconductor devices, n.e.c. in chapter 90
Equipment	841459	Fans; n.e.c. in item no. 8414.51
	841950	Heat exchange units not used for domestic purposes
	842129	Machinery for filtering or purifying liquids, n.e.c. in item no. 8421.2
	842139	Machinery for filtering or purifying gases, other than intake air filters, catalytic converters or particulate filters for internal combustion engines
	842199	Machinery parts for filtering or purifying liquids or gases
	848620	Machines and apparatus of a kind used solely or principally for the manufacturing of semiconductor devices or of electronic integrated circuits
	848640	Machines and apparatus of a kind used solely or principally for the manufacturing or repairing of masks and reticles, assembling semiconductor devices or electronic integrated circuits, or for lifting, handling, loading or unloading items of heading 8486
	848690	Machines and apparatus of heading 8486; parts and accessories thereof
Output	8542	Electronic integrated circuits and microassemblies
	852351	Semiconductor media; solid-state non-volatile storage devices, whether or not recorded, excluding products of Chapter 37
	852352	Semiconductor media; smart cards, whether or not recorded, excluding products of Chapter 37
	852359	Semiconductor media; other than smart cards, whether or not recorded, excluding products of Chapter 37
	853290	Electrical capacitors; parts of the capacitors of heading no. 8532
	8533	Electrical resistors (including rheostats and potentiometers), other than heating resistors
	8534	Printed circuits

(*Continued*)

Appendix 4.1 (Continued)

Step 3: The use of semiconductors in intermediate electronics		
Raw Materials	*Output from Step 2*	
Inputs	8540	Thermionic, cold cathode or photo-cathode valves and tubes, e.g. vacuum or vapour or gas filled valves and tubes, mercury arc rectifying valves and tubes, cathode ray tubes and television camera tubes; parts thereof
	854110	Electrical apparatus; diodes, other than photosensitive or light-emitting diodes (LED)
	854121	Electrical apparatus; transistors, (other than photo-sensitive), with a dissipation rate of less than 1W
	854129	Electrical apparatus; transistors (other than photo-sensitive), with a dissipation rate of 1W or more
Output 1: Intermediate Industry	851190	Ignition or starting equipment and parts (heading no. 8511), for use in spark-ignition or compression-ignition internal combustion engines
	852729	Radio-broadcast receivers for motor vehicles, not capable of operating without an external source of power and not combined with sound recording or reproducing apparatus
	854430	Insulated electric conductors; ignition wiring sets and other wiring sets of a kind used in vehicles, aircraft or ships
	901210	Microscopes (excluding optical microscopes); diffraction apparatus
	901290	Microscopes (excluding optical microscopes); diffraction apparatus; parts and accessories
	901490	Navigational instruments and appliances; parts and accessories
	902490	Machines and appliances; parts and accessories for those testing hardness, strength, compressibility, elasticity or other mechanical properties of materials (e.g. metal, wood, textiles, paper and plastics)
	902790	Microtomes and parts and accessories thereof
	902890	Meters; parts and accessories of gas, liquid, electricity supply or production meters, including calibrating meters thereof
	902990	Meters and counters; parts and accessories for revolution and production counters, taximeters, mileometers, pedometers and the like; speed indicators, tachometers (excluding heading no. 9015), stroboscopes
	903090	Instruments, apparatus for measuring, checking electrical quantities, not meters of heading no. 9028; parts and accessories, for measuring or detecting alpha, beta, gamma, x-ray, cosmic and other radiations
	903190	Instruments, appliances and machines; parts and accessories for those measuring or checking devices of heading no. 9031

(*Continued*)

Appendix 4.1 (Continued)

	903290	Regulating or controlling instruments and apparatus; automatic, parts and accessories
	903300	Machines and appliances, instruments or apparatus of chapter 90; parts and accessories n.e.c. in Chapter 90
Output 2: Intermediate Consumer	8473	Parts and accessories (other than covers, carrying cases and the like) suitable for use solely or principally with machines of headings 8469 to 8472
	851761	Base stations
	851762	Communication apparatus (excluding telephone sets or base stations); machines for the reception, conversion and transmission or regeneration of voice, images or other data, including switching and routing apparatus
	851769	Communication apparatus (excluding telephone sets or base stations); machines for the transmission or reception of voice, images or other data (including wired/wireless networks), n.e.c. in item no. 8517.6
	851890	Microphones, headphones, earphones and amplifier equipment; parts of the equipment of heading no. 8518
	852290	Sound or video recording or reproducing apparatus; parts and accessories thereof, other than pick-up cartridges
	852990	Reception and transmission apparatus; for use with the apparatus of heading nos. 8524 to 8528, excluding aerials and aerial reflectors
	9006	Photographic cameras, photographic flashlight apparatus and flashbulbs (excl. discharge lamps of heading 8539)
Step 4: Production of final electronics incorporating semiconductors		
Input	*Output 1 and 2 from Step 3*	
Output 1: Final Industry	8470	Calculating machines and pocket-size data recording, reproducing and displaying machines with calculating functions; accounting machines, postage-franking machines, ticket-issuing machines and similar machines, incorporating a calculating device; cash registers (excl. data-processing machines of heading 8471 and automatic goods-vending machines)
	8471	Automatic data processing machines and units thereof; magnetic or optical readers, machines for transcribing data onto data media in coded form and machines for processing such data, n.e.s.
	8472	Office machines (e.g. hectograph or stencil duplicating machines, addressing machines, automatic banknote dispensers, coin-sorting machines, coin-counting or wrapping machines, pencil-sharpening machines, perforating or stapling machines, n.e.s.)

(*Continued*)

Appendix 4.1 (Continued)

	8526	Radar apparatus, radio navigational aid apparatus and radio remote control apparatus
	9014	Direction-finding compasses; other navigational instruments and appliances (excl. radio navigational equipment)
	9022	Apparatus based on the use of x-rays or of alpha, beta or gamma radiations, whether or not for medical, surgical, dental or veterinary uses, including radiography or radio-therapy apparatus, x-ray tubes and other x-ray generators, high tension generators, control panels and desks, screens, examination or treatment tables, chairs and the like
	9027	Instruments and apparatus for physical or chemical analysis (e.g. polarimeters, refractometers, spectrometers, gas or smoke analysis apparatus); instruments and apparatus for measuring or checking viscosity, porosity, expansion, surface tension or the like; instruments and apparatus for measuring or checking quantities of heat, sound or light (including exposure meters); microtomes; parts and accessories thereof
	9028	Gas, liquid or electricity supply or production meters, including calibrating meters thereof; parts and accessories thereof
	9029	Revolution counters, production counters, taximeters, milometers, pedometers and the like (excluding gas, liquid and electricity meters); speed indicators and tachometers (excluding those of heading nos. 9014 and 9015); stroboscopes
	9030	Instruments, apparatus for measuring, checking electrical quantities not meters of heading no. 9028; instruments, apparatus for measuring or detecting alpha, beta, gamma, x-ray, cosmic and other radiations
Output 2: Final Consumer	851712	Telephones for cellular networks or for other wireless networks
	851718	Telephone sets n.e.c. in item no. 8517.1
	851770	Telephone sets and other apparatus for the transmission or reception of voice, images or other data, via a wired or wireless network; parts
	851810	Microphones and stands therefor
	852580	Television cameras, digital cameras and video camera recorders
	8528	Monitors and projectors, not incorporating television reception apparatus; reception apparatus for television, whether or not incorporating radio-broadcast receivers or sound or video recording or reproducing apparatus
	9006	Cameras, photographic (excluding cinematographic); photographic flashlight apparatus and flashbulbs other than discharge lamps of heading no. 8539
	950450	Games; video game consoles and machines, other than those of subheading 9504.30

Source: OECD, "Measuring distortions in international markets: The semiconductor value chain", OECD Trade Policy Papers 234, 2019.

Notes

1 Commonly known as "back-end manufacturing", ATP entails transforming silicon wafers produced by front-end fabs into finished chips ready to be fitted into electronic modules and final devices. ATP activities are often outsourced to specialist firms that slice finished silicon wafers into individual chips, package them into protective shells and test for defects before shipping them to electronics manufacturers. Back-end manufacturing is less capital-intensive and employs vastly more labour than front-end manufacturing.

2 "Emerging Resilience in the Semiconductor Supply Chain", Report by BCG-SIA, May 2024.

3 Malaysia currently accounts for 13% of the global market for semiconductor packaging, assembly and testing and is aiming to boost that to 15% by 2030. "Exclusive: Chinese firms look to Malaysia for assembly of high-end chips, sources say", Reuters, 19 December 2023.

4 "Taiwan and the global semiconductor supply Chain: Global semiconductor policy and development", *Monthly Report* (August/September 2025) by Taiwan Representative Office in Singapore.

5 Henry Yeung et al., "From fabless to fabs everywhere? Semiconductor global value Chains in transition", *Global Value Chain Development Report 2023*, World Trade Organisation.

6 OECD, "Measuring distortions in international markets: The semiconductor value chain", OECD Trade Policy Papers 234, 2019.

7 "Mapping global supply Chains: The case of semiconductors", *Rabobank*, 15 June 2023.

8 Calculations from UN Comtrade database.

9 Author's calculations from UN Comtrade database.

10 Although sufficiently disaggregated trade data are not available, anecdotal evidence suggests that the high-end lithography machines needed to manufacture leading-edge semiconductors (<10 nanometres) are almost entirely produced by one Dutch company, ASML. Refer to OECD, "Measuring distortions in international markets: The semiconductor value chain", OECD Trade Policy Papers 234, 2019.

11 Refer to source in Endnote 2. Taiwan notably dominates high-end semiconductor fabrication, producing many of the world's most advanced logic chips. South Korea focuses on both logic and memory semiconductors.

12 Studies have found that countries which have increased their electronics exports to the United States after the spike in US tariff have also increased imports of electronics from China, indicating the rerouting of goods via third countries to circumvent trade barriers. Freund, et al., "Is US trade policy reshaping global supply Chains?" World Bank Policy Research Working Paper Series 10593, 2023. Laura Alfaro and Davin Chor, "Global supply Chains: The looming 'Great Reallocation'", NBER Working Paper No. w31661, September 2023.

13 "The New Jedi Order: global chip war and the semiconductor industry", Allianz Research, 6 March 2025.

5 Geopolitics and Global Value Chain in East Asia (II)

Rivalry and Technological Competition

Heightened US Export Curbs on Technology to China

The United States has introduced the most sweeping restrictions on technology exports on China since the Cold War. In October 2022, it unilaterally announced strict export controls and licensing requirements on semiconductor technology, with the aim of preventing American firms from supplying Chinese entities with high-end chips and the tools, technology and software to design and produce them. In March 2023, Japan and the Netherlands followed suit without explicitly referencing China, by announcing new export controls on key semiconductor technology, effective from July 2023.

The export controls, targeting areas such as advanced semiconductors (both logic or memory chips), and other chips used in supercomputing and artificial intelligence (AI) were further tightened in 2023. With the Foreign Direct Product Rule (FDPR), the United States could exercise extraterritorial jurisdiction, restricting items produced abroad if they contain US-origin components or technologies. In December 2024, these controls were further expanded to include High-Bandwidth Memory (HBM), a type of memory that is critical for AI applications. This covers a new chokepoint which aimed to impede China's indigenous development of AI hardware.[1] In addition, the list of restricted semiconductor manufacturing equipment (SME) was updated to include tools for producing HBM, DRAM and advanced packaging.

The Biden administration had embraced the term "small yard, high fence" to describe its technology controls affecting China – in other words, the universe of restricted technologies could be comparatively small, but the restrictions will be extremely stringent.[2] The goal is clearly to slow China down and blunt its capabilities in cutting-edge areas by weaponising key chokepoints such as AI chips, electronic design automation software, manufacturing equipment and related components. To ensure its leading position in critical supply chains such as semiconductors, the United States has singled out (or "blacklisted") Huawei and other

DOI: 10.4324/9781003674221-5

Chinese high-tech firms, such as ZTE and Semiconductor Manufacturing International Corporation (SMIC) (refer to Appendix 5.1), in its techno-nationalist innovation race with China. These companies have been denied access to the US telecommunications market and subjected to stringent export controls.[3]

China's Patchy Leap in Chip Manufacturing

The impact of the highly prohibitive export controls is potentially far-reaching and hard-hitting as China's semiconductor industry is heavily reliant on overseas suppliers, mainly from the United States and Japan (such as Applied Materials, Lam Research and Tokyo Electron) for tools for advanced nodes. Due to US export controls on China since October 2022, the three main firms, such as SMIC, Yangtze Memory Technologies (YMTC), ChangXin Memory Technologies (CXMT) and other Chinese chip manufacturers, are forced to use less-advanced technologies/equipment for production, putting them at a competitive disadvantage in the logic and DRAM segments.[4]

Notably, in a recent development, the United States' export ban on advanced semiconductors has also reportedly delayed the launch of China's artificial intelligence (AI) company DeepSeek's latest model R2, due to its use of Huawei's product rather than Nvidia's server chips.[5] DeepSeek was encouraged by the Chinese authorities to adopt homegrown technology after releasing its R1 model in January 2025. However, it has encountered hurdles in training its R2 model with Huawei's Ascend processor, highlighting the challenges China faces in attempting to supplant US technology.

Given the stringent US export controls, China has adopted a more pragmatic solution of first establishing itself in mature nodes (28 nm for logic chips and for memory) by capitalising on its existing advantages in mass production, namely scale economies from its huge domestic market, large industrial clusters, a large pool of engineers and a dynamic ecosystem in key sectors such as 5G related chips, Internet of Things and automotive chips.[6]

Driven by state industrial policies promoting the localisation of chip production and development, China has invested heavily in mature-node semiconductor production in recent years. According to the Semiconductor Industry Association, China's share of global mature-node semiconductor capacity more than doubled from 19% in 2015 to 33% in 2023.[7] By contrast, Japan's share of global mature-node semiconductor production capacity fell from 19% to 15% while that of Europe declined from 15% to 14% over the same period.[8]

China's spending on both chip plant construction and chipmaking equipment has surged due to the generous government subsidies and support from investments from large state-led funds, such as the China Integrated Circuit Industry Investment Fund. As Chinese OEMs making smartphones, cars or computers are increasingly concerned about supply chain disruptions from US-led export controls, this has fuelled demands for "in China for China" production.[9] China's chipmaking capacity, as measured by the number of 8-inch wafers that can be processed by its fabrication plants, has increased dramatically, making it the global leader (Figure 5.1).

According to the latest available data, China accounted for around 31% of global legacy chip production at the end of 2023, up from 17% in 2015, and is set to widen its lead with more planned fabs for mature node production. Projections from Taiwanese semiconductor research firm *TrendForce* show that China will likely account for 39% of global legacy capacity by 2027.[10]

Chinese production remains heavily concentrated in legacy chips, also known as mature chips or mature nodes, which are less-advanced semiconductors used in a wide array of electronic devices ranging from household appliances to electric vehicles.[11] In automotive chips, China's SMIC operates at process nodes as advanced as 14 nm for European automotive chipmakers, generating good returns that support investment in advanced or next-generation chips.[12] As seen in Figure 5.2, China has essentially no production capacity for high-end chips, a market segment dominated by firms in Taiwan, Korea and the United States.

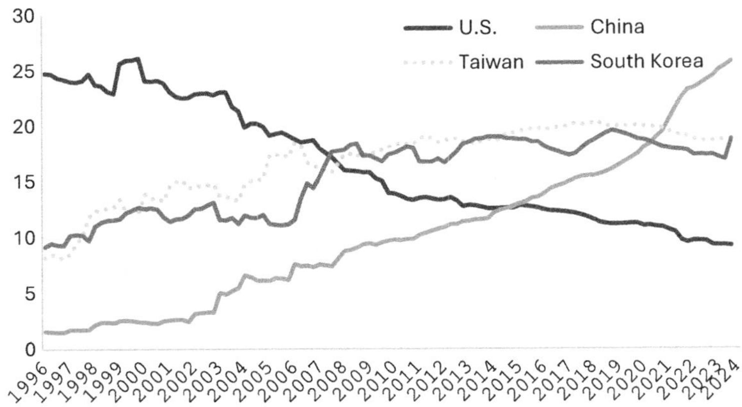

Figure 5.1 Global wafer capacity, 1996–2023.

Sources: Gartner, SEMI World Fab Forecast Gartner, US Fed Reserve.

Note: Data extend through 2023:Q3.

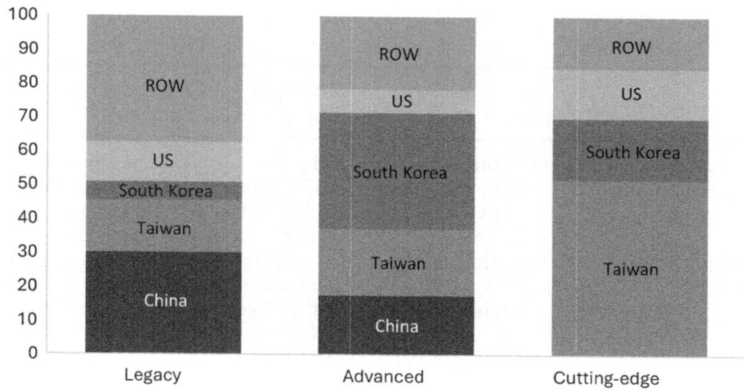

Figure 5.2 Capacity by node group.

Sources: SEMI World Fab Forecast; US Federal Reserve.

Note: Legacy nodes are 28 nm and above, advanced nodes are 6 to 27 nm, and cutting-edge nodes are 5 nm and below. ROW = rest of the world.

Table 5.1 shows the entry barriers and US restrictions across various chip segments. Generally, lower-end semiconductor segments at 28 nm and above, such as general-purpose logic chips and automotive microcontrollers, face lower entry barriers. Entry barriers for NAND chips are not as high as that for DRAM chips. The main players are Samsung and SK Hynix from South Korea. Samsung, the leading firm, produces 12-nm chips (DDR5), whereas SK-Hynix has recently taken the lead in the new HBM segment.[13] China's CXMT trails behind, producing 16-nm chips with lower technological sophistication.[14]

In the NAND chip segment, there are more producers, reflecting a somewhat lower degree of entry barriers. The key players are Samsung and Hynix, but China's Yangtze Memory Technologies Corp has somewhat caught up with the leading firms in South Korea in terms of technological level by producing 232-layer chips (Table 5.1). In logic chips, the leading firm is TSMC. Both TSMC and Samsung Foundry are expected to begin mass production of 2-nm chips in the second half of 2025 in Taiwan and South Korea, respectively.[15]

The wide-ranging US sanctions have severely hindered China's efforts to progress into more leading-edge chip making areas, including the manufacturing process, equipment manufacturing, or advanced design software and tools. Table 5.1 shows strict US export restrictions on semiconductor technologies to China, specifically targeting technologies and equipment used in manufacturing logic chips below 18 nm, DRAM below18 nm and NAND memory chips of 128 or more layers.[16] Despite

Table 5.1 Various chip segments: Entry barriers, frontier technologies and US restrictions

	DRAM memory chips	*NAND flash memory chips*	*Logic chips (processors)*
Usages (conventional examples only)	Computers, servers, graphics cards and AI data centre	USB and solid-state drives and tablets	Diverse applications from smartphones and PCs to cars and servers
Entry barrier	Very high; need EUV for high productivity	Not that high; no need for EUV (Deep Ultraviolet Lithography or DUV is sufficient)	Depends on segment (low end)
Global Frontier (i.e. leading firms)	DDR5 at 12 nm (Samsung/ Micro)	238 layers (SK Hynix)	2 nm (TSMC)
US restrictions	No to 18 nm or less	No to 128 layers or more	No to 16/14 nm or below
China's frontier (firms)	16 nm in 2022 (CXMT)	232 layers in 2022 (YMTC)	14 nm commercially viable volume production; 7 nm volume production with dubious yield rate in 2022 (SMIC)
Factories in the United States by East Asian firms (in planning stage or under construction)	No plant by any Asian firm	Samsung's old plant in Austin, Texas	4 nm: Samsung in Texas (US$25 billion, delayed to 2025); 4 nm: TSMC (Arizona in 2024); 2 nm (Arizona in 2028)

Source: Refer to source in Endnote 4.

these stringent US "chokepoint" measures against China, leading domestic firms in China have achieved a certain degree of technological catch-up.

In August 2023, Huawei launched its 5G-capable Mate 60 Pro handset with far more China-made components than previous models (one-third or so), suggesting that China is making progress in localising semiconductor supply chains.[17] The smartphone uses a 7-nm chip, marking a breakthrough for SMIC, which manufactured these chips without access to EUV lithography machines. However, producing advanced chips with older equipment is more time-consuming and costly.[18] China has relied on DUV lithography equipment stockpiled in China before the ban took effect. Restrictions on China's access to EUV machines have thus effectively prevented Chinese firms from mass producing advanced-node chips at the scale or efficiency of leading global players like TSMC or Samsung.[19]

China is generally considered to be two or three generations behind global leaders such as Taiwan and South Korea in the high-end segment of chip making.[20] In the DRAM chip segment, advanced generations of DRAM chips at 12–14 nm require EUV lithography equipment to cramp more transistors onto the same wafer layer containing multiple DRAM chip cores (Table 5.1). Producing NAND chips, on the other hand, does not require EUV lithography and require less-advanced lithography method (e.g. DUV systems).[21]

Nevertheless, Chinese firms have shown significant innovation capacity and made rapid progress in patent generation, particularly in HBM, an advanced type of DRAM optimised for AI applications and high-performance computing. Industry insiders note that HBM production does not necessarily require cutting-edge EUV lithography and is believed to be less challenging than producing DRAM chips at nodes below 10 nm. As a result, China can produce its own HBM chips at the 17–19-nm node without the latest equipment.[22] Moreover, HBM technology stacks memory cells vertically, necessitating advanced (high-density) packaging technologies such as through-silicon-via (TSV), a field where China is relatively advanced.[23]

Given that HBM can be developed without EUV lithography, ChangXin Memory Technologies (CXMT) has reportedly started mass production of second-generation HBM2.[24] At the time of this writing, although CXMT still lags behind SK Hynix, Samsung and Micron which are already producing advanced HBM3 and HBM3e chips and planning for HBM4 production, this nonetheless represents a major step forward in China's efforts to reduce its reliance on foreign suppliers. This advancement is particularly noteworthy amid ongoing tensions with Washington and restrictions on US exports of advanced chipsets to China.

While China has made rapid progress in the number of patents, particularly in logic chips, it still lags behind South Korea and Taiwan in DRAM patents. It faces challenges in commercialising patents given the existing restrictions in accessing vital technologies and equipment, like EUV or even DUV, and advanced software. Currently, lithography is the biggest chokepoint and the least localised sector in China's semiconductor supply chain, where China relies almost exclusively on a handful of foreign suppliers, such as ASML of the Netherlands.[25]

Hence, China's chances of leapfrogging in advanced chipmaking depend largely on its access to and progress in lithography equipment.[26] If China were to close the technological gap in advanced semiconductors, one view is to use DUV rather than EUV systems to produce sufficiently advanced chips, and the other is to develop EUV equipment domestically.

In March 2023, Shanghai Micro Electronics Equipment, China's leading producer of lithography equipment, filed a patent for EUV scanners, underscoring China's progress in its efforts to develop indigenous EUV technology. Yet the journey from filing a patent to commercialising a product is lengthy and complex, and puts China behind global leaders such as ASML which has already advanced to High-NA EUV technology, further widening the gap between China and its competitors.[27]

It is highly unlikely, if not impossible, at least in the near future, to replicate the EUV systems, given the extreme and systematic complexity of EUV lithography.[28] To replicate the EUV machine requires longtime collaboration with critical global suppliers. For instance, despite ASML being the only supplier of EUV machine in the world, its development of the EUV is the result of more than two decades of collaboration between ASML and its many highly sophisticated partners around the world; it still relies on a highly globalised network of some 5,000 suppliers to build the machine, many of whom are dominant or even sole suppliers in their respective fields.[29]

Responses from South Korea and Taiwan

The curbing measures imposed by the United States on China have somewhat limited the sales of semiconductor-related goods to China from Korea and Taiwan. The restrictions have created risks for Korean and Taiwanese firms operating fabs in China. These export controls prevent the import of advanced equipment like the new EUV equipment for their fab operations in China. In October 2022, Samsung and Hynix were granted one-year waivers from such restrictions, with further exemptions granted in October 2023. Despite this, Samsung and Hynix still face competition from Chinese firms ramping up production of general-purpose chips. As China is an important market and closing the fabs is not viable, the two South Korean memory chipmakers are significantly reducing their production of legacy memory chips, particularly DRAM, amid falling prices caused by greater output from Chinese companies.[30]

As a result of geopolitical risks, Samsung and Hynix are expanding their domestic fabs in South Korea. Similar to Samsung which has not invested its core products of DRAM chips overseas,[31] Taiwan's TSMC has so far retained the high-end gigafabs at home and low-end fabs abroad. It has separated its fabs serving the US and China markets based on the sophistication and process technologies for different chips. For instance, TSMC's fabs in China (Nanjing and Shanghai) are producing and supplying lower-end logic chips to fabless customers in China, whereas high-end chips for US fabless firms such as Apple, AMD and Nvidia are produced in home gigafabs in Taiwan.

US restrictions on Chinese firms' access to critical advanced technologies have in a way benefitted Taiwan by slowing China's progress in developing state-of-the-art logic chips, allowing Taiwan to dominate in high-end chip manufacturing. However, concerns remain that China could influence the market towards the use of less-advanced chips in many applications.[32] With its expanding and large domestic market for consumer electronics, automotive and smart devices, it could incentivise OEM firms to use lower-end chips in these products, potentially reducing demand for higher-end chips and services from Taiwan. This is particularly a concern for smartphone processor chipmakers such as MediaTek and NAND memory chip producer Phison Electronics.[33]

Taiwan is also under pressure to build more chipmaking fabs in the United States, given the importance of the US market as major sources of chip demand (by Apple and Nvidia). Government incentives further encourage investment in advanced chip fabrication in the United States. However, the concern is with the inefficiency of such a move as regions like Phoenix, Arizona, where TSMC fabs are located, lack the necessary workforce and infrastructure for advanced semiconductor manufacturing.[34] This may limit TSMC's productivity in wafer fabrication. Ironically, chips produced in US fabs will still need to be tested and packaged in Taiwan before shipment to US customers, resulting in higher costs compared to those manufactured domestically.[35]

Shortly after the United States threatened to impose tariffs on Taiwan in February 2025, TSMC announced plans to invest at least US$100 billion over the next few years to build state-of-the-art semiconductor manufacturing facilities in the United States. This has led to serious concerns within Taiwan that TSMC's substantial investment in the United States would undermine the strategic vital semiconductor industry.[36]

Managing Geopolitical Currents

Strengthened US restrictions on technologies to China have already affected American semiconductor companies like Qualcomm which have lost revenue and market share in China.[37] The restrictions also affect semiconductor-manufacturing equipment produced in Singapore and Malaysia. As a major exporter of semiconductor manufacturing equipment to China, Singapore could see its exports subject to the Foreign Direct Product Rule depending on the proportion of US-origin components or technologies they contain.

In early August 2025, US President Trump threatened to impose 100% sectoral tariffs on imported semiconductors unless there is substantial investment in the country. Smaller chip firms such as UMC and Vanguard would be disadvantaged if the tariff is broadly applied. There would be wider negative repercussions on supply chains and rising costs for semiconductor firms in the region, including Singapore. At the time of this writing, details remain vague as to how the tariff would be implemented, whether Singapore-based chip firms with US origins or semiconductor-related products shipped indirectly to the United States could be taxed, for instance.

Further, Southeast Asian economies like Vietnam which ship integrated circuits to China could be affected. Companies are under increased pressure to exercise due diligence in terms of compliance with US export controls in order to avoid being blacklisted or risk losing export privileges (to the United States) and banks' access to credit and trade financing. This could increase operational and production costs and impact profits, thereby reducing the attractiveness of investing in Southeast Asia's semiconductor industry. Not aligning with the US export controls could also undermine the country's ambitions to be a global data centre hub if the companies are blacklisted by the United States. Malaysia, for instance, has imposed a strategic trade permit requirement on exporters in July 2025 to tighten oversight of the movement of AI chips from the United States and seek to clamp down on potential diversion of AI chips to third countries.[38]

The geopolitical tensions between the United States and China may force Asian firms to navigate a complex landscape of export controls and sanctions, complicating their supply chains. One major Taiwanese firm in the testing and packaging segment, namely King Yuan Electronics Co, reportedly said it would exit the mainland China market, underscoring the increasingly difficulties that firms face in navigating a more complicated geopolitical climate.[39]

To ensure compliance with US regulations, TSMC, for instance, reportedly took a cautious approach and decided that it would not ship orders to its clients that utilise foreign chip packaging suppliers' facilities in China, regardless of whether it is on the US "white list" of approved businesses.[40] This is regardless of whether the chips are for artificial intelligence applications or for other uses. The move has reportedly dealt a major blow to Chinese chip developers as unapproved chip packaging suppliers would force them to change providers in order to procure chips made by TSMC. Testing and chip packaging firms in Southeast Asia like Malaysia or Vietnam may inadvertently benefit.

China's huge semiconductor market presents a paradox to American and foreign chip companies. Despite geopolitical tensions, China is hugely attractive to firms like Qualcomm or Intel as China accounted for over 30% of worldwide chip sales in 2022.[41] To maintain revenue or market share in the lucrative market, some firms have adopted the strategy of selling older technologies to China while not contravening US export restrictions. Nvidia, for instance, modified or re-designed two AI chips A800 and H800 for the China market to comply with US export rules, since its most advanced AI chips, the A100 and H100, were banned for use by Chinese companies. It reportedly also plans to export the H20 chip to China.[42] The H20 is less powerful than Nvidia's top-of-the-range semiconductors, and the United States has lifted the ban on this AI product as part of the trade deal with China to resume its rare earth exports. Resuming H20 chip sales would allow Nvidia to slow down its competitor Huawei which has sold its own AI chips to Chinese developers who are unable to access H20 due to the ban.

The tech rivalry between the United States and China is not expected to ease anytime soon, even if both sides negotiate to de-escalate trade tensions. Considering historical precedents, the outcome of the US-China trade war could be quite different from that of the US-Japan trade war in the 1980s, whereby Japan's semiconductor industry lost competitiveness after the country was pressured into signing the US-Japan Semiconductor Agreement in 1986. Unlike Japan, which is more willing to compromise due to its historical dependence on the United States for military security, China is less reliant on the United States and is in an economically stronger position to resist US pressure compared to Japan's limited leverage in the past. This resulted in Japan having comparatively limited bargaining power to counteract the United States. As the United States continues its technological confrontation, China is more likely to push back and challenge US hegemony, unlike Japan's inability to settle the trade dispute on its own terms.

Appendix 5.1 Broad-based technology and semiconductor restrictions on China

Date	*Selected actions and measures by the United States*
Feb 2020	The United States bans government purchases of Huawei gear.
Jun 2020	US Federal Communications Commission (FCC) designated Huawei and ZTE as national security threats to communications network.
Mar 2021	US FCC blacklisted five Chinese telecom companies: Huawei Technologies Co, ZTE Corp, Hytera Communications Corp, Hangzhou Hikvision Digital Technology Co and Dahua Technology Co.
Apr 2021	US Commerce Department blacklisted seven Chinese supercomputing entities: Tianjin Phytium Information Technology, Shanghai High-Performance Integrated Circuit Design Centre, Sunway Microelectronics, National Supercomputing Centre Jinan, National Supercomputing Centre Shenzhen, National Supercomputing Centre Wuxi and National Supercomputing Centre Zhengzhou.

(*Continued*)

Appendix 5.1 (Continued)

Date	*Selected actions and measures by the United States*
Apr 2021	US Senate Foreign Relations Committee approved the Strategic Competition Act of 2021, which mandates diplomatic and strategic initiatives to counteract Beijing.
Jun 2021	US Senate passed the Innovation and Competition Act of 2021 to address challenges posed by China by fostering US scientific research on technological innovation, especially in semiconductors and cybersecurity.
Oct 2021	US FCC revoked China Telecom America's services authority.
Nov 2021	The United States blacklisted over a dozen Chinese quantum computing companies including Shanghai Quantum CTek and Hefei National Laboratory for Physical Sciences at the Microscale. In addition to quantum computing, the list included companies in the semiconductor and aerospace industries.
Dec 2021	The United States added Chinese artificial intelligence company SenseTime on its investment blacklist.
Dec 2021	US Treasury Department blacklisted eight Chinese technology firms, including drone maker DJI Technology Co Ltd. The US Commerce Department adds 24 more Chinese entities to its "entity list".
Feb 2022	US House of Representatives passed America Competes Act, which addresses pressing economic issues facing the Biden administration, including supply chain disruptions and global shortage of semiconductor chips. Additionally, the bill calls for changes to US trade rules to level the playing field for American businesses and combat China's so-called market-distorting trade practices.
Mar 2022	The US Securities and Exchange Commission (SEC) released a list of five Chinese companies including Baidu for possible delisting from US stock markets. It added Weibo to a list of Chinese companies for possible delisting from the US stock exchange.
May 2022	The US SEC added over 80 firms, including China's JD.com to a list of entities facing possible expulsion from American exchanges amid a long-running auditing standoff between the United States and China.
Jul 2022	The US SEC added Alibaba Group to the list of Chinese companies at risk of being delisted if they failed to show their audits to US regulators by Spring 2024. Shortly afterwards, five of China's largest state-owned enterprises – China Life Insurance, PetroChina, China Petroleum and Chemical Corporation, Aluminium Corporation of China and Sinopec Shanghai Petrochemical – announced plans to delist from the New York Stock Exchange.
Aug 2022	The United States passed the CHIPS and Science Act.
Aug 2022	The United States added another seven China entities, mostly related to aerospace, to its export control list.
Oct 2022	The Department of Commerce's Bureau of Industry and Security (BIS) issued two new rules on restricting US and foreign firms for shipping high-end microchip manufacturing equipment to China.

(*Continued*)

Appendix 5.1 (Continued)

Date	*Selected actions and measures by the United States*
Oct 2022	The United States added China's Yantze Memory Technologies Co (YMTC) and 30 other Chinese entities to the "unverified list" (i.e. a list of companies that US officials have been unable to inspect).
Oct 2022	The United States announced restrictions on US citizens and green card holders working for certain Chinese semiconductor and AI companies.
Dec 2022	The United States announced ongoing talks with Japan and the Netherlands to restrict advanced chip exports to China.
Dec 2022	US Congress proposed bill to add Huawei and other Chinese telecom companies to Treasury "specially designated nationals" list. It also proposed ban on Chinese-linked social-media platform TikTok.
Feb 2023	Department of Commerce added six Chinese entities to a sanctions list for their support of China's military efforts.
Mar 2023	Department of Commerce added 28 Chinese companies to "entity list" to restrict their ability to purchase American technology due to concerns about their involvement in activities deemed contrary to US national security interests.
Apr 2023	Department of Commerce imposed export controls on 12 more Chinese companies, restricting their access to American technology due to concerns about potential national security risks related to advanced computing and military applications.
Aug 2023	President Biden issued executive order restricting US investments in Chinese technology sector.
Oct 2023	The United States further tightened export controls of advanced chips to China.
Mar 2024	US House of Representatives passed bill to ban TikTok.
Apr 2024	President Biden signed bill that will force ByteDance to divest from TikTok.
May 2024	The United States was set to increase tariffs on Chinese electric vehicles, solar panels, semiconductors following review of Sec. 301 tariffs starting August 2024.
Jun 2024	US Treasury issued draft regulations restricting US investment in sensitive technology sectors in China.
Sep 2024	US Commerce Department implemented export controls for Quantum computing and other advanced technologies.
Sep 2024	House of Representatives passed several bills targeting Chinese companies and industries, primarily restricting their presence in the US market. Among these, the Biosecure Act barred federal support for biotechnology companies that collect Americans' genetic data. The five Chinese companies targeted were BGI Group, Complete Genomics, MGI, Wuxi AppTec and Wuxi Biologics.
Sep 2024	US Trade Representative finalised China Sec. 301 tariff actions following a four-year review.
Oct 2024	US Treasury added two Chinese entities to the Specially Designated Nationals (SDN) list. The entities were Shenzhen Boyu Imports and Exports Co. Ltd. and Shenzhen Jinghon Electronics Limited. Being added to the SDN list subjects the firms to sanctions, restricting their access to the US financial system and prohibiting US persons from engaging in transactions with them.

(*Continued*)

Appendix 5.1 (Continued)

Date	*Selected actions and measures by the United States*
Oct 2024	The United States issued final rules on investment restrictions against China targeting semiconductors, AI and quantum computing.
Nov 2024	US advisory panel recommended revoking China's Permanent Normal Trade Relations (PNTR) status.
Dec 2024	The United States further expanded chip export controls and added 140 Chinese companies, many of which make the tools and machinery necessary for manufacturing chips, to the "entity list" (a restricted trade list).
Jan 2025	President Biden unveiled new curbs on exporting advanced Nvidia AI chips.

Source: MUFG, "Trade War 2.0 Will Be Different", February 2025 and various news sources.

Notes

1 Rhodium, "Slaying self-reliance: US chip controls in Biden's final stretch", 9 December 2024.
2 "Balancing the ledger: Export controls on U.S. chip technology to China", *Centre for Strategic and International Studies*, 21 February 2024.
3 Henry Yeung et al., "From fabless to fabs everywhere? Semiconductor global value Chains in transition", *Global Value Chain Development Report* 2023.
4 Chan-Yuan Wong et al., "Geopolitics and the changing landscape of global value chains and competition in the global semiconductor industry: Rivalry and catch-up in chip manufacturing in East Asia", *Technological Forecasting and Social Change*, (209), 2024.
5 "DeepSeek's next AI model delayed by attempt to use Chinese chips", *Financial Times*, 14 August 2025.
6 Refer to source in Endnote 4.
7 SIA analysis on SEMI, "World Fab Forecast", 20 December 2024.
8 SIA analysis on SEMI, "World Fab Forecast", 20 December 2024.
9 Rhodium, "Thin ice: US pathways to regulating China-sourced legacy chips", 13 May 2024.
10 "China's legacy chips to survive with price advantage", *Asia Times*, 21 March 2024.
11 US export controls define legacy chips as those larger than the "16- to 14-nm" generation. Chips of this size are slightly more than a decade old. "China is poised to dominate the market for legacy chips, and the U.S. may only have itself to blame", *Fortune*, 6 July 2024.
12 Caines, Colin, Sharon Jeon and Cheyenne Quijano, "Developments in Chinese chipmaking", FEDS Notes, Washington: Board of Governors of the Federal Reserve System, 17 January 2025.

13 Refer to source in Endnote 4.
14 "Global chip race: China semiconductor sector surpasses South Korea", *TechWire Asia*, 12 March 2025.
15 "Samsung, TSMC set stage for fierce race in 2 nm chip tech", *The Korea Herald*, 15 June 2025.
16 Refer to source in Endnote 4.
17 Refer to source in Endnote 4.
18 Simply put, using DUVs for the 7-nm process requires more manufacturing steps to fit in as many transistors as possible on each chip. Lithography, a crucial step in chipmaking, is the process of transferring highly complex electrical circuit patterns onto silicon wafers. EUV machines can set patterns on a wafer using only a single exposure, while DUV machines require three or four rounds of patterning for a 7-nm chip. Multi-patterning increases complexity and reduces precision, while consuming more time, materials and components.
19 Although there are 7- and 6-nm chips being made in limited quantities using older deep ultraviolet technology, the volumes are low and yields are uneconomical. Deloitte, "2025 global semiconductor industry outlook", 4 February 2025.
20 Alex He, "In the global AI chips race, China is playing catch-up", *Centre for International Governance Innovation*, 18 September 2024.
21 Refer to source in Endnote 4.
22 Shilov, Anton, "Chinese DRAM maker developing HBM-like memory", *Tom's Hardware*, 30 August 2023.
23 Refer to source in Endnote 4.
24 Currently, only SK Hynix, Samsung and Micron can make advanced HBM chips (HBM3 and HBM3e). They are preparing to advance to HBM4 in the coming years. TrendForce, "ChangXin Memory Technologies in China Has Reportedly Begun Mass Production of HBM2", 6 August 2024.
25 Refer to source in Endnote 4.
26 Refer to source in Endnote 4.
27 "Taiwan and the Global Semiconductor Supply Chain – China's Pursuit of Semiconductor Self-Sufficiency", Monthly report (April/May 2025) by Taipei Representative Office in Singapore.
28 "China's chipmaking breakthrough too good to be true", *Caixin*, 23 September 2023.
29 For example, Carl Zeiss of Germany is ASML's only supplier of precision mirror systems, one of the most critical optical parts for the EUV machine, while San Diego-based Cymer, which ASML acquired in 2013, is the sole provider of the EUV light source. "ASML says decoupling chip supply chain is practically impossible", *Financial Times*, 27 June 2023.
30 "SK Hynix, Samsung to cut legacy DRAM output as Chinese firms catch up", *The Korea Economic Daily*, 1 November 2024.
31 Almost 75% of DRAM memory chips globally are made in South Korea. Refer to Lino Jeng, "DRAM market dynamics – February 2024", *Omdia*, 26 February 2024.

32 Refer to source in Endnote 4.
33 Refer to source in Endnote 4.
34 Refer to source in Endnote 4.
35 Refer to source in Endnote 4.
36 "Why concern is growing in Taiwan about chip giant TSMC's pledge to invest in Arizona", *SCMP*, 8 March 2025.
37 Qualcomm, for instance, derives approximately 65% of its revenue from China. Micron receives over 50%, while almost all major US tech firms from Intel to Texas instruments derive approximately 20% to 40% of global revenues from China. Alex Capri, "Strategic US-China decoupling in the tech sector", Hinrich Foundation, 2020.
38 "Malaysia tightens domestic oversight of US chip movements as tariffs negotiation tactic", *The Straits Times*, 14 July 2025.
39 "Geopolitics and U.S. rules push chip firms to decouple from mainland China, with one major Taiwanese testing company ditching the market entirely", *Fortune*, 30 April 2024.
40 "U.S. chip curbs hit China harder than expected as TSMC treads carefully", *Nikkei Asia*, 8 February 2025.
41 Alex Capri, *Techno-Nationalism: How It's Reshaping Trade, Geopolitics and Society*. John Wiley & Sons, 2024.
42 "Nvidia shares climb as White House relaxes export rules on China chip", *Financial Times*, 15 July 2025.

Index

Pages in *italics* refer to figures, pages in **bold** refer to tables, and pages followed by n refer to notes.

For Product Safety Concerns and Information please contact our EU representative GPSR@taylorandfrancis.com Taylor & Francis Verlag GmbH, Kaufingerstraße 24, 80331 München, Germany

Printed and bound by CPI Group (UK) Ltd, Croydon, CR0 4YY
14/09/2026
02216256-0001